D0559543

The Journey of

T. D. JAKES

The Journey of
T. D. JAKES

Living a Life of Faith, Blessing, and Favor

RICHARD YOUNG

THE JOURNEY OF T. D. JAKES:
Living a Life of Faith, Blessing, and Favor

Richard Young
P.O. Box 272282
Oklahoma City, OK 73137
e-mail: youngsr@sbcglobal.net
www.now-gochangeyourworld.org • www.rickyoung.us

ISBN: 978-1-60374-069-2
Printed in the United States of America
© 2008 by Richard Young

Whitaker House
1030 Hunt Valley Circle
New Kensington, PA 15068
www.whitakerhouse.com

Library of Congress Cataloging-in-Publication Data

Young, Richard, 1952–
  The journey of T. D. Jakes / by Richard Young.
    p. cm.
  ISBN 978-1-60374-069-2 (trade hardcover : alk. paper) 1. Jakes, T. D. I. Title.
  BX8762.5.Z8J39 2008
  289.9'4092—dc22
  [B]
                        2008024778

1 2 3 4 5 6 7 8 9 10 11 12 ᵂᴴ 16 15 14 13 12 11 10 09 08

DEDICATION

This book is dedicated to my uncle,

REV. HOMER L. YOUNG,

who pastored churches in Oklahoma for nearly sixty years, and to all of the other people who have served the Lord faithfully all of their lives with very little notice from much of the world around them. Uncle Homer loved the Lord and yearned to reach souls for the kingdom of God.

Homer answered the call as a young man and then reached out to his brother, Waldo, my father, who also answered the call. He shepherded churches and sang gospel music for the rest of his life. As one of the hardest working men I have ever known, he was up before dawn every morning to spend time in the Word and with his Lord. After breakfast with his family, he went out to reach others for Jesus.

He passed away a few months ago, less than thirty days after he had last gone door-to-door, witnessing to people and inviting them to the small church where he was preaching. He was singing gospel music with his two brothers less than a week before he died. He entered heaven, was greeted by the Lord, and was immediately engulfed by the many people he had led to the Lord.

> *Therefore, since we are surrounded by such a great cloud of witnesses, let us throw off everything that hinders and the sin that so easily entangles, and let us run with perseverance the race marked out for us. Let us fix our eyes on Jesus, the author and perfecter of our faith, who for the joy set before him endured the cross, scorning its shame, and sat down at the right hand of the throne of God.*
>
> (Hebrews 12:1–2 NIV)

ACKNOWLEDGMENTS

I would like to acknowledge people without whom this book would not exist.

My wife Brenda, who is more than my helpmate and companion. She encourages me and helps me find the words when I am so tired I can't think. She is truly my missing rib.

My three children Rick Jr., Athena, and Amy, as well as their spouses, Pam, Paul, and Brent. I thank the Lord every day for their faith. They pray for their father every day and that strength helps me so much.

My nine grandchildren: Annamarie, Rebecca, Abigail, Brandon, Paige, Benjamin, Faith, Levi, and Naomi. They keep me young, even while reminding me that I am getting older. Some have already accepted the Lord, and I pray for the others to find Him as they grow in knowledge.

My parents, Waldo and JoAnn Young, my in-law parents, Wilfred and Elsie Listen, and my sisters and brother-in-law, Sharon, Ed, and Annette—my family has been faithful to follow the direction of the apostle Paul: *"And the things you have heard me say in the presence of many witnesses entrust to reliable men who will also be qualified to teach others"* (2 Timothy 2:2 NIV). My children are now following this direction as well.

I would also like to acknowledge the support of Charles and Frances Hunter. Frances has been a strong mentor to me and encouraged me to write. Bob and Christine Whitaker, and my editor, Tom Cox, of Whitaker House—they are the people who have helped make my dreams come true.

Finally, my Lord and Savior, Jesus Christ. It is my daily prayer to bring honor to Him in all that I do.

—*Richard Young*

CONTENTS

PREFACE

I believe there are a number of pastors and evangelists making a difference in this country and throughout the world. These are men and women gifted by God to touch people with the gospel of Jesus Christ. There is no pattern to the background, doctrinal orientation, education, or ethnicity of the effective pastor. They are Baptists, Pentecostals, Methodists, charismatics, or have no denomination whatsoever. They are young and old. But there is one thing they have in common: they have an anointing to reach the world for Jesus Christ.

T. D. Jakes is one of those people. In many ways, he is no different from thousands of preachers across the country, who toil in ministry, working side jobs to make ends meet, all for the privilege of following the call of God on their lives. Every so often, however, God seems to reach down and raise up one of His servants to the attention of the world. T. D. Jakes has laid down his life to touch his community for Jesus Christ. Agree with him or not, it is hard to argue that as Jakes has been faithful to the cause of the gospel, God seems to have blessed and honored that faithfulness. Those blessings, however, have not come free of both criticism and controversy.

This book is an attempt to document the meteoric rise of Jakes's life and ministry. It is not my goal to sit in judgment of the man's words, methods, or doctrine. Similarly, it is not my goal to roundly justify or validate every move he has made. Rather, it is my intent to examine Jakes's triumphs as well as his trials that we might better understand him and the clarion call that God has on his life. In doing so, I hope to acknowledge both his fans and his critics, those whose lives he has changed and those who watch him with a wary eye, that the reader would gain a great appreciation for the undeniably incredible journey he has undertaken.

Today, God continues to honor the tireless labor of the faithful men and women who serve Him around the world. Many will do so in obscurity all of their lives. They will never write a best seller, produce a successful Hollywood movie, or counsel presidents, but they are making an eternal difference in His kingdom. This book is to honor and encourage them in their calls. To them, I hope this book says, "God sees what you are doing, and He will honor your faithfulness as well."

Let us not grow weary while doing good, for in due season we shall reap if we do not lose heart.   (Galatians 6:9)

—Richard Young

1

"GET READY!"

People see me on TV as a preacher and they say, "We don't know what else he's doing, gosh golly. He wears a bunch of suits and he's got a diamond ring on his finger and who is he?" But the secret to what I do is not what you see on TV.

—T. D. Jakes[1]

Chapter One

"Get Ready!"

Get ready! Get ready! Get ready!"

All around the auditorium, people are standing and shouting, some cheering as if at a sports stadium, others rocking back and forth as tears stream down their cheeks. On the platform, a tall, broad-shouldered, dark-skinned man with a gap-toothed smile stands wearing an immaculate suit and gripping a white handkerchief as he once again shouts these words.

"Get ready! Get ready! Get ready!"

On this Sunday, as most others, thousands have streamed in from all over the Dallas/Ft. Worth metroplex and beyond to hear this man preach the Word of God. As his booming voice soars, it reverberates around the room and rattles in your chest. Then, in an instant, it drops to a whisper, and the entire crowd seems to lean forward in an effort to catch every word. Whether or not you agree with his message, no one can doubt the charisma that flows from Bishop T. D. Jakes.

This is The Potter's House, Jakes's church, which claims 30,000 members. What began in 1994 as a church of roughly fifty families in West Virginia has quickly blossomed into a multiracial, nondenominational congregation, and one of the fastest growing and most influential churches in America. Largely composed of African-Americans (roughly 77 percent), the rest of the congregation is Caucasian, Hispanic, and a variety of other nationalities. In 2005, *Time* magazine included Jakes in its list of the twenty-five most influential evangelicals, just four years after it dubbed him "America's Best Preacher." His annual revival, MegaFest, had drawn over one hundred thousand people. His annual women's conference, Woman, Thou Art Loosed, spawned a best-selling book and was adapted into a successful commercial motion picture starring T. D. Jakes as himself.

LIFE PREPARATION

Everything T. D. Jakes does, from preaching to writing to leadership development, has the specific intention of preparing people for life. Unlike many preachers, whose primary intention seems to be preparing people for eternity, Jakes knows that people also need to be able to face life today. To that end, Jakes seems to recognize and tap into a deep and very practical need for help in facing the daily struggles of relationships, raising children, pursuing a career, and paying the bills. As *Charisma* magazine editor Lee Grady says, "He taps into the core of human weakness and need and then proclaims Christ as an answer to that, in a way that causes people to stand up and shout."[2] It's easy to tell someone to simply "let go and let God." It's much more complicated to lead someone to the place where he or she can experience God's practical, day-to-day help in facing the trials of life.

> Everything Jakes does, from preaching to writing to leadership development, has the specific intention of preparing people for life.

Preaching these messages may seem easy to some, but dealing with real issues about real people can get messy. Jakes deals with sexual relationships between unmarried people at a time when some churches don't want to ask couples if they are married or not. He doesn't, however, simply wag his finger, pronounce the evils of sin, and move on. Instead, he acknowledges that there are strong and beckoning temptations in our society. While he seems to empathize with those who struggle daily against the pull of the world, he also talks about how to resist those lures and get beyond them.

Jakes talks about the problems that many face in their marriages. He speaks to women who are disrespected and abused by their husbands, verbally or physically, and reminds them that they do not need to view such behavior as acceptable in a relationship. He encourages people to work out their problems and persevere through difficult times, but he also states that people do not need to live in desperation. God does not expect people to live lives of misery and despair; He wants them to live lives of abundance. This, he says, is as true of our relationships as it is of every other area of life.

Another issue he frequently addresses is preparing parents to raise children in a modern society. Jakes does not shy away from tackling the issue of young men wearing pants that droop down to their thighs and young women dressing provocatively. T. D. preaches fearlessly, unafraid of chasing young people off by speaking the truth. He empowers parents to stand strong as role models for their children and as the source of authority and order in the home. He proclaims that if things in society and culture are going to change, there must be changes within the next generation. Our children must be challenged to meet high standards in their academic endeavors and in their personal behavior, and to seek and maintain only relationships that are beneficial to them in every way. Jakes says that he wants to raise the expectations of both the parents and children for what the future can hold and how that future can be achieved. In doing so, he works to help both parents and children get ready for the life that is ahead of them.

Jakes also helps people deal with the challenges of life in the workplace. Most people spend more time at their jobs and on their commutes to and from work than they spend with their families. It is not uncommon for people to spend ten or eleven hours a day away from home. The success or failure people experience at work has a direct impact on every part of their lives. Jakes deals with the traits and tools that can lead to success or failure at work. He teaches his congregation practical steps toward obtaining and keeping good jobs. He talks about the important role that education plays in preparing individuals for successful careers. He also discusses nontraditional educational opportunities, such as finding a mentor or looking for the right professional conferences, that will provide a chance to network with others who have been successful.

Paying the bills is another subject he addresses from the pulpit. Jakes talks about making wise decisions when making purchases, both major and minor. He details the role of establishing good credit and of building long-term assets for the family. He talks about credit cards—how they can be useful and how they can be destructive. He explains the

> God does not expect people to live lives of misery and despair; He wants them to live lives of abundance.

importance of buying a home to build equity and long-term assets. He explains how the equity in a home can be used as a foundational asset to purchase investment property or to obtain the needed capital to start a business. Jakes's goal is to change people's mind-sets from those of day-to-day survival to those of long-term success where anyone can actually become a creator of wealth.

T. D. Jakes's goal is to see God transform the lives of the people in his congregation and other congregations where he speaks, changing their lives for eternity. In that vein, he believes that people should start reaping the benefits of God's wisdom and power from this day forward, not just after they die. He desires people to think generationally—and not simply day-to-day—and then pass that wisdom on to the next generation. He quotes the apostle Paul: *"The things that you have heard from me among many witnesses, commit these to faithful men who will be able to teach others also"* (2 Timothy 2:2).

For T. D. Jakes, it has been a long and winding journey to where he stands today. Listen to his messages and you will hear snippets of those early days. You will hear of sermons preached in little clapboard churches located "across the tracks." You'll hear of places where the definition of air conditioning was a hand fan from the local funeral home and a strong right arm, and places where turning up the sound meant raising your voice. The Potter's House was built to be an example of what a church could be, using the latest technology. But Jakes is not far removed from another place and another time—a bygone era and a people who recognized the call of God on his life, encouraged his gifts, and shaped the attitude he has today.

As much as anything else, it is that attitude that creates the atmosphere of The Potter's House—an attitude suggesting that great things are going to happen. For many in his congregation who have never before experienced such an atmosphere in a church, this attitude is contagious. They buy T. D. Jakes's books, listen to his CDs, go to his conferences, and keep coming back to The Potter's House no matter how long the drive.

But how did something so big happen so fast to someone so unlikely? This may be the story of The Potter's House, but it is also the story of that attitude of expectancy and victory. It is *The Journey of T. D. Jakes.*

JAKES FAMILY VALUES

My mother was a woman of faith and conviction. She definitely helped to secure my belief in God. But she was not a sweet, sappy, super-spiritual saint who carried her Bible everywhere she went and greeted people with "Praise the Lord." No, she was a real person with real challenges—and she had a real faith in a real God....It was like bedrock beneath every obstacle she ever faced, every emotion she ever felt, every decision she ever made, and every victory she ever gained. She did not flaunt it, she did not spiritualize it, she simply lived it.

—T. D. Jakes[3]

Chapter Two

JAKES FAMILY VALUES

On June 9, 1957, in South Charleston, West Virginia, Ernest and Odith Jakes welcomed a son, Thomas Dexter Jakes, into the world. Their humble home was nestled into the rich, robust Appalachians where plush greenery accentuated the rolling peaks of the mountainous terrain. "Tommy" Jakes grew up entertaining himself by running up and down the trails and scenic paths of the countryside, splashing in the creek beds, singing songs, and reveling in "preaching" sermons to any rock, tree, or furry animal along the way.

ODITH JAKES

T. D. Jakes was born into a family that was unique in ways that would lay the foundation for who and what he was to become.

His mother, Odith, was one of fifteen children. Not only did her parents have fifteen children of their own, but they also took in seven other children from their extended family. They wanted these children to have opportunities they would not have had otherwise. Odith's parents were role models for what good Christian parents should be.

Odith attended Lincoln High School in Marion, Alabama, where she was a classmate and fellow choir member with Coretta Scott, who would later become the wife of Martin Luther King Jr. Odith would often tell the family about Coretta's beautiful singing voice, something

T. D. would discuss with Bernice King, the daughter of Coretta Scott King, many years later.

Odith's parents instilled strong values in their children and the other children they cared for. They created ambition in them, and a drive to be successful in life. Eventually, Odith graduated from one of America's most prestigious African-American schools of higher education, Tuskegee University.

Trained as a home economics teacher, Odith taught all of her children to cook, clean, and sew. Long before their first day of formal education, she also made sure that all three of her children were able to read and insisted that they learn poetry, especially the works of black poets. Before Tommy Jakes entered the first grade, he could recite James Weldon Johnson's "Lift Every Voice and Sing," often referred to as "the black national anthem." Odith taught her children the works of African-American writers like Ralph Ellison, Langston Hughes, and others. She made certain that her children never saw themselves as victims, regardless of the circumstances around them. She also taught them that education does not begin in a classroom but is a lifelong process.

> Odith Jakes taught her children that education does not begin in a classroom but is a lifelong process.

Tommy Jakes was the youngest of the three children, and he was very close to his mother. As a small child, he would follow closely behind her. As a highly respected educator in the community, she was often invited to speak at luncheons and banquets for various groups. Jakes once told his mother that although he went with her now when she spoke, the time would come when she would go with him when he was the speaker.

Today, Jakes has strong and positive memories of his mother, describing her as "bionic." He recalls how she could clothe and feed her entire family while staggering with a fever. She could bake a birthday cake without an electric mixer while talking on the phone. She could cook a roast in a broken oven. He describes how she would take twenty-five dollars and a bus ticket and go to the grocery store with her three children in tow. Later, having stretched that money into a week's worth of groceries, she would still cook dinner before five o'clock, even without packaged food or processed meats.[4]

One of Odith's prized possessions was a curio cabinet that she called "the china cabinet." In it were the finest glasses, plates, and silverware the family owned. Every member of the family knew that they were *never* to take a glass from that cabinet to use for water or milk. Odith cherished that piece of furniture and the things inside it. Anyone disturbing the cabinet or its contents would face her wrath. Jakes would later use that cabinet as an illustration when speaking about vessels of honor and vessels of dishonor.[5]

It is obvious from the memories that Jakes often shares of his mother that they were very close and that their relationship has impacted every facet of his life.

ERNEST JAKES

Ernest Jakes's family faced a great many more challenges than Odith's did. His parents, Thomas Dexter and Lorena Jakes, lived in rural Mississippi at a time when Jim Crow laws and the Ku Klux Klan were active in the Deep South. When Ernest was a child, and while his mother was expecting her second child, his father drowned. At the time, his death was officially determined to be an accident. Later, however, it was discovered that he had actually been murdered. The river where he drowned was a place where he often went swimming as a shortcut for getting to work. Apparently, he had been "advised" by some white men to stop swimming in the river but chose to ignore their warning. Later, barbed wire was discovered in the river directly in the path where he often swam. It was speculated that he had become entangled in the barbed wire while swimming and had drowned. Eventually, the current had freed his body from the wire, and he was discovered.

Despite losing her husband—and the family breadwinner—Ernest's mother chose not to be bitter. Instead, she continued to work their farm, raise her children, and do everything in her power to better their lives. Eventually, she graduated from college as a middle-aged woman and then remarried. Through it all, she was an example of resilience and dignity to her children and grandchildren.

While his own children were young, Ernest Jakes often held down two or three jobs at a time. Because of this, he saw very little of his children, but, like his mother, Ernest was a man driven to provide opportunities for his children. Today, it is hard to imagine the world in which Ernest Jakes lived, especially for those who did not live as people of color in the segregated America of the 1950s and 60s. In some areas, it was not only difficult for a black man to get ahead in life, but there were even laws against it!

> In some areas, it was not only difficult for a black man to get ahead in life, but there were even laws against it.

As a child, Tommy Jakes did not always appreciate how his father had to work long hours for little pay so there would be food on the table and a roof over their heads. He knew that his father worked virtually around the clock, but, as a child, he simply thought that his father did not want to be bothered by his children. In the foreword to one of T. D. Jakes's books, Odith wrote about how hard it was at that time for a black man in West Virginia to make a living, having to work hard while making certain that he did not offend the white society around him. It was only with hope, faith, and great vision that black families were able to encourage their children to envision a society of equal opportunity that did not yet exist.

THE NUCLEAR FAMILY

In many ways, Tommy Jakes lived an idyllic life as a child. He was part of a true "nuclear" family—with both parents, siblings, and even a family dog, Pup. T. D. recalls waking up on Sunday mornings to the smell of waffles filling the house. In worn pajamas, he would follow the aroma to the kitchen for a family breakfast at a small Formica table with rusty legs.

Raised in rural West Virginia where family and faith were a way of life for both blacks and whites, Jakes spent much of his boyhood in the little town of Vandalia. To the locals, it was simply known as "up the hill." To get there, you would drive up Mountain Road, a steep, winding pathway with numerous little dead-end streets branching off in all directions. Theirs was a neighborhood of a split-level, wood frame houses divided racially by a large, green water tower—whites on the north side of the tower; blacks on the south side.

The black community was very closely knit, perhaps due to the fact that there were only about fifty families at that time. Everyone knew each other and watched after each other's children and property. It was very much an extended family. If anyone was in need, neighbors would be there to help out as best they could. They were aware of the hopes and ambitions of each other's children. They kept track of how successful they were in school and what they wanted to be when they grew up.

By this time, the Jakes family consisted of five—two boys, Ernest Jr. and Tommy, and a girl, Jacqueline, along with mom and dad. Ernest Sr. had been raised African Methodist Episcopal, but circumstances led the family to a Baptist church, a denomination that was much more prominent in the Charleston area among the African-American community. Tommy attended Sunday school each week, where he was taught the Word of God. Now, around fifty years later, Jakes still describes his childhood Sunday school teacher as the best Christian he has ever known.[6] Mrs. Inez Strickland taught the children their Bible verses. She used an old piano with only half its keys working to teach them songs to sing. She took care of children who were ailing and even visited them when they were out sick. For Tommy Jakes, this was a Christian who lived her faith every day of her life.

On Sunday afternoons, Odith would pack lunches and the Jakes family would pile into their 1957 red and white "rust bucket" of a Chevrolet and drive leisurely through the countryside. It was cheap entertainment for a black family in the early 1960s, but it also allowed them to see their world as more than the four walls of their small home. Ernest Jakes wanted his children to see more than he had seen, to hope for things he never had the chance to obtain, and to do things he would never do. Like most fathers, he wanted his children to experience a better life than he had.

T. D. Jakes was still a child as American society was in the early stages of the civil rights movement. *Brown v. Board of Education* had been decided. Central High School in Little Rock, Arkansas, had been integrated. Rosa Parks had refused to move to the back of the bus.

West Virginia had sided with the North during the Civil War—the very reason it had separated from Virginia. It existed on the edge of the South but was not a part of the *Deep* South. However, many of its values and beliefs were still embedded in Southern culture. Yet, it was on those Sunday afternoon drives that Ernest and Odith Jakes could open the eyes and dreams of their children without intruding upon or offending the sensibilities of the white society around them.

THE EARLY YEARS

When Tommy Jakes was five, he was large for a kid his age. As the baby of the family, he was excited to start attending school. He saw it as a rite of passage to be a part of the "big kid" ritual of getting ready and boarding the bus each day. There was just one obstacle to this passage. In the middle of the path between his house and the bus stop was a very large rock. On either side of the rock were patches of thorny blackberry bushes. The other kids in the neighborhood were smaller and more nimble and would easily scamper over the rock. It might as well have been Mount Everest to big ol' Tommy Jakes, however, who became completely paralyzed with fear whenever he came to the base of the rock. Each day he would run down the path, certain that this would be the day he would climb the rock, and each day he would end up crying until his mother or father came down the path to help him over.

Perhaps fed up with this routine, Ernest finally took a mallet and pick to the rock and carved steps into it. Now, instead of having to climb over the rock, Tommy was able to step over it effortlessly. What had been an obstacle in his life had been made into a victory. Tommy's father had come through for him that day and become a "superhero."

Odith Jakes raised her children to take the prospect of the kingdom of God seriously. Neighbors remember how young Tommy Jakes didn't always play outside like other kids—preferring, instead, adult company. In a community that placed heavy emphasis on churchgoing and worship, Tommy Jakes gravitated toward several deeply religious adults. In a CNN interview, Jakes shared, "I carried the Bible in school and they called me the Bible Boy and the Boy Preacher."[7]

"He was a really smart boy," recalls Bobbie Tolliver, a neighbor who was close to the family. "He tried hard to prove to everybody that he was going to be someone someday."[8] Even in those early days, Tommy Jakes seemed to realize that he had a higher calling.

A CHRISTMAS WISH

One Christmas, Tommy Jakes wanted a very special present. It was much more, however, than the typical Christmas wishes of a young boy—a bike or a football. Tommy wanted a piano. He had seen the used, upright piano in the window of the Arbogast piano store in South Charleston. He told his mother about this special Christmas wish and did everything he could to prove how sincere he was.

Finally, he convinced his mother to go with him to visit the object of his affection. At the store, Tommy touched the instrument with great respect. He admired it. He gushed over it. He told his mother how much he wanted to play the piano and how perfect it would be. He told her that he already knew three songs, almost, and would learn many more if he had a piano of his own on which he could practice. Tommy was well aware that this was a very big gift. He knew of his family's financial situation. That's why he tried to be realistic in asking for a *used* piano.

On Christmas morning Tommy went downstairs with great anticipation, hoping against hope that his dream gift would be next to the tree. He looked around the tree but there was no used upright piano. Instead, there was a *brand new*, beautiful, mahogany console piano! It took his breath away. He could hardly believe that his parents loved him so much that they were willing for the entire family to sacrifice so that he could have the object of his dreams.[9]

True to his word, Tommy Jakes practiced that piano nearly every day. It proved to be the beginning of his later calling as a young music director at a small Baptist church. He also used the piano in his first pastorate when he was older.

FAMILY WORK ETHIC

The work ethic of the Jakes family established habits and a drive in Jakes that are still with him to this day. He tells stories of his Mississippi grandmother working to gather the eggs from the henhouse, feed the mule, and milk the cow when the sun was coming up. She then turned her attention to the garden, singing hymns and spiritual songs in the morning air. It was work that some might consider drudgery. Yet Jakes's grandmother was appreciative of hard work and looked forward to the rewards it would provide, and she taught Tommy to do the same.

T. D. Jakes is a fifth-generation descendant of slaves. As a child he got to know his great-grandmother, Nancy Jakes, the daughter of a former slave. Ever since slavery, however, many in the Jakes family had been entrepreneurs. T. D. often reflects on the business sense he witnessed as a child. "My Mama was into real estate for years. I grew up in a home where they talked about business."[10] Ernest and Odith let their children know that success did not come easily but through hard work. It was made clear that no matter the color of their skin or the circumstances around them, they could make something of themselves.

> Ernest and Odith let their children know that success did not come easily but through hard work.

Wanting to follow the example of his parents, Tommy had a series of small jobs and entrepreneurial efforts as a child. Jakes still tells of working in neighbors' gardens under the hot West Virginia sun, weeding and hoeing in the dirt. He speaks of the immense satisfaction from seeing the vegetables come to harvest and selling them around the neighborhood. His sister, Jacqueline, later described his sales efforts: "When he was very young, he would bag up collard greens and take them around the neighborhood and sell them for maybe a dollar a bag."[11] Working in the gardens also taught him the biblical principle of sowing and reaping. He knew from working in the gardens as a child that if you plant bean and squash seeds, you will harvest beans and squash. Whatever you plant will come back to you in kind.

Tommy worked at all the typical jobs that young boys did, such as a paper route, mowing the neighbor's lawn, and anything else he could do to earn money. He also had an unusual job for a boy—he sold Avon to the ladies in the neighborhood. At one point he was able to save fifty dollars from his efforts—a great deal of money for anyone at that time. He used the money to buy his mother a new coat. He thought it was the most beautiful thing he had ever seen and something his mother never would have splurged on for herself.

Building a Business

All those years of hard work began to pay off for Ernest Jakes, as he was able to take a mop and a bucket and build a successful custodial business. At its peak, Ernest employed over fifty people and cleaned everything from grocery stores to the state capital. For a man of color to build a successful company at this time was quite a feat. He also kept some side businesses going, even cleaning a few places after normal business hours that were not really clients of the cleaning company. He did this so that no matter what else happened in his life, he would have money coming in to ensure that he would always be able to care for his wife and children. Ernest's management style was very much "hands on." He did not go home to his family until every job was not only completed, but also performed at a professional level that met the high standards he had established.

Eventually, Ernest Jakes was able achieve his lifelong dream of building a new home for his family. He was even able to afford some of the luxuries that few families could at the time, including a dishwasher and patio. It's easy to take these things for granted today, but such luxuries were extremely rare in black communities at the time.

Ernest Jakes had what many would regard as the ideal family. He had two teenaged children and a younger son, all of whom loved and respected their parents. They were good kids who loved God and did well in school. Ernest Jakes was well respected in both the black and white communities, and was the spiritual leader of his family. He understood that financial prosperity was not enough; he also had to impart spiritual values to his children. Each night, he would sit at the head of the table and say grace in a rich, baritone voice: "Father, we thank you for the food that we are about to receive for the nourishment of our bodies. In the name of the Lord Jesus Christ we pray, amen."[12]

ADVERSITY STRIKES

With his father becoming a successful businessman and his mother an educated teacher, the Jakes's family was better off than the vast majority of African-Americans of their generation. It was the plan of Ernest Jakes to pass the prosperity he had attained to his children. He hoped to live a long life and then to hand his company over to his youngest son, Tommy. This, however, was not to be. When Tommy Jakes was just ten years old, his perfect family situation began to fall apart when his father was diagnosed with kidney disease.

Ernest had taken a physical to do some work for a prestigious company in West Virginia. They immediately recommended that he go to a specialist at the Cleveland Clinic. He spent weeks at the clinic, and when he came home, he was weak, fatigued, and had lost a great deal of weight.

Unaware that he had suffered from high blood pressure his entire life, which had slowly destroyed his kidneys, Ernest had never gone to the doctor unless he'd been ill to the point that he could not work. For years he had suffered from hypertension, which had been exacerbated by factors of weight and stress. In a few short months, the Jakes's family prosperity began to slip away into a world of expensive medical bills and less and less family income.

Later, T. D. would write,

He was gone in a flash—not dead, not yet anyway—but he was gone. The vibrancy, the life, the strength, and the stamina were gone from him. He had finally built his dream house and had established his company, but now he was so sick he couldn't enjoy it.[13]

Odith Jakes immediately began to spend every moment of her time taking care of her husband as well as trying to be the breadwinner for the family. She continued to teach, but the loss of her husband's income, combined with the new medical expenses to combat his disease, placed tremendous pressure on the family's financial stability.

By this time, both of T. D.'s siblings, Ernest Jr. and Jacqueline, were grown and had left home to pursue their own lives. Jacqueline left home at seventeen, almost immediately after she graduated from high school, for the widely paved boulevards of Washington, D.C. This placed a huge responsibility on Tommy's shoulders and created an even greater bond with his mother.

During the six years of Ernest's illness, Odith depended upon Tommy to help out in ways that most young teens would not be able to accept. Suddenly, his prosperous and carefree childhood gave way to adult responsibilities and concerns. He became responsible for much of his father's care. As he grew older, he also became the family bookkeeper, making sure all the bills were paid. He quickly became comfortable dealing with people in a business environment as he received a practical education that would serve him well throughout his life. Odith Jakes did not have the knowledge or time to run her husband's business. Thus, by the time Tommy Jakes was thirteen, he was the one who opened and closed his father's shop, as well as the one who hired, fired, and paid the employees. Slowly, he began to see himself as a successful businessman and assumed that this was a role he would play for the rest of his life.

GROWING UP TOO SOON

Tommy Jakes's life had changed dramatically. The little boy who did not know how to ride a bike quickly learned how to operate a dialysis machine. He would later say,

> I grew up suspended somewhere between life and death, shaving and bathing my father, mopping up blood that spilled from the

dialysis apparatus, sleeping in hospital corridors, watching my mother work too many hours and go without much as I watch my father's health dwindle to death. If my father was sick, we'd lay him in the back seat of the car and turn the emergency lights on, and my mother would drive and I would take care of him till we got to the hospital. If there was an emergency and she screamed out my name, I came running—she was clamping off his shunts...I can still see it. I will always be able to see it. I can draw a picture of the kidney machine, virtually.[14]

Even as he assumed the role of an adult, he was still a teenager who dealt with the hormones and challenges that teens face, and who would occasionally test his mother's rules. On some nights, he would sneak out of the house after carefully placing pillows in his bed to make it look as though he was asleep. After a full night of sneaking around, he would sneak back in the house shortly before breakfast only to learn the hard way why his mother had forbidden him to stay out: he was exhausted from his exploits and had no energy left for his day! He eventually learned that his mother's rules were not to stop him from enjoying life; they were to help him enjoy his life.

THE TEEN YEARS

The 1960s were a turbulent and changing time in American history. Not only were civil rights a major issue of the times, but the drug culture was also making its presence known. The hippie movement was encouraging young adults to "tune out and turn on." Musicians, both black and white, were adopting the drug culture and modeling its values.

For about a year or so, Tommy followed suit, chasing economic opportunity by selling "nickel bags" ($5) of marijuana to his fellow junior high classmates. Recently, when pressed on the issue, he said, "Believe me, that was not unusual at the time."[15] Jakes was a teenager with adult-sized responsibilities. His father was ill and expenses were piling up as the family's income was falling. As a result, Tommy felt compelled to contribute in any way he could. Though this activity went on for only a short time, from this experience, Jakes seems to understand firsthand how desperate situations will sometimes lead well-meaning people to take desperate measures.

In the last years of his life, Ernest Jakes ate food that tasted like cardboard and drank cranberry juice—a natural cure for urinary tract infection—by the gallon. He followed all of his doctor's orders to the letter. Yet, it did not make a difference in his condition. Ernest Jakes died an excruciatingly slow death and Tommy witnessed nearly every moment of it. He tells of watching his once robust father go from 280 pounds to a mere 130, until he was nothing more than skin and bones. Ernest would sit in their home and spend hours watching life pass by outside the patio window that he was so proud of. During the last moments of his life, doctors were beating on his chest, trying to get his heart, destroyed by renal failure and illness, to beat one more time. Ernest Jakes was only forty-eight when he died.

The only positive thing to come from Ernest Jakes's illness was that it gave him the time to bond with his youngest son. When healthy, he had worked long hours to provide for the family. When Ernest Jakes was on his deathbed, he said something profound to his son that has stayed with T. D. all of his life. "Son, I want you to know something. By the time I figured out what life was really all about, it was time to go."[16]

Tommy Jakes had the opportunity to know his father in a way that his brother and sister never had. Ernest's death deeply disturbed and angered Tommy, but it also caused him to vow that he would never allow life to stop him from having a strong relationship with his children.

After Ernest Jakes's death, his body was taken to Mississippi to be buried alongside his family. Tommy Jakes stood beside his father's grave as a sixteen-year-old boy who had grown up too quickly. As the dark brown casket was dropped into the ground, he stood there wearing adult clothes—a black suit, blue shirt, and yellow tie. In his heart, however, he was still a little boy, desperately desiring his father's approval, hoping that he had assumed the responsibilities and performed the tasks for the family in a way that his father would approve of. Jakes says that the day he dropped his father into the Mississippi clay was the most difficult day in his life. "To some degree, I felt like a failure because I wanted him to live so bad, and I had dedicated most of my youth to trying to keep him. When he died I was devastated."[17]

> ## What T. D. did inherit from his father was a desire to achieve.

Tommy Jakes's father did not leave him much in the way of material possessions—just a watch and a ring. Neither of these items had much monetary value. What he did inherit from his father, however, was a desire to achieve. In a relatively short period of time, Ernest Jakes had achieved a certain level of prosperity for his family. He believed that through hard work and applying himself, he could accomplish more than what others were able to. Rather than work a typical job for someone else, Ernest built a business that created jobs for other people. If Ernest Jakes had not been struck down by disease before he was fifty years old, he would have achieved even more success in his life. He was definitely on the way up.

As he dealt with the illness of his father and assumed the responsibilities he had to accept, Tommy reached out to his heavenly Father in a way uncommon for most young people. His father was ill and his mother was busy. His brother and sister had their own lives and responsibilities. But this proved to be a great blessing. He had the opportunity to grow in the Lord, and he used the time during his father's illness to develop some spiritual traits that would help him in his later life and ministry. Instead of being self-centered, He learned the value of sacrifice. During the illness, his father's needs came first because his life depended upon it. Tommy developed an inner drive to do more, achieve more, and be more than others.

This drive to achieve came partially from his mother, as well, who taught him that the whole world is a university, that everyone in it is a teacher, and when you wake up in the morning you have to be sure that you go to "school." Tommy Jakes quickly picked up the baton and continued the route of achievement.

Today, one wonders if Jakes desires achievement as a reflection of what could have been had his father lived longer. He all but confessed this fact in his book, *Maximize the Moment*, writing that there comes a time in a person's life when a desire is created to get "there." He says his father was headed "there" when he died, and now he is heading toward the same place. According to Jakes, "there" is different for everyone, but we must all strive to get to our "there."

ONE MORE DETOUR

During Tommy's senior year in high school, Odith Jakes was diagnosed with stomach tumors. Once again, he was forced to take on adult responsibility, quitting school to care for his mother. He later said, "I can remember looking out the window and saying, 'I can't do this twice,' you know. It was a tough year, but I was going to be there for her."[18]

Tommy's mother was seriously ill and he wanted to be near her. He had already lost one parent, and he wasn't about to lose another. For her part, Odith was not happy about her son quitting school. As a lifelong teacher, she held completing an education in high esteem. Tommy, however, felt he had no other choice.

For a while, during his mother's illness, he took a job in a local paint store. Later, he took a job at a chemical plant owned by Union Carbide, where he worked as a processor of oxygen and acetylene. In Charleston, this seemed like a great opportunity, and Jakes had every reason to believe that working at the plant would provide a middle-class lifestyle for him and whoever the Lord would provide for a wife. Little did he know that the end was near for big-time manufacturing in the Rust Belt section of the United States.

Life certainly might have turned out differently for Tommy Jakes if his father had lived and taken his son into the family business. Things also might have taken another route had the job at Union Carbide not dried up. What is certain is that God had another calling in store for Thomas Dexter Jakes.

A HIGHER CALLING

After his father died, things at his home began to return to a type of normalcy. Tommy was able to reassume the role of a teenager, but he seemed caught in the midst of an internal conflict. His body was that of a teenager, but in many ways his soul had emotionally grown up as he had assumed the various roles and responsibilities of a man. Subtly, Tommy Jakes began to feel a call from God on his life.

He accepted a part-time position in the music ministry of the small Baptist church he had grown up in. There, he was known to gather up the children and teens of the neighborhood and drag them down to the church for long choir rehearsals. West Womack was one of those teens. He describes himself at that time as a "hard head," someone whom Tommy had to hunt down and drag to the church. Most of the time, West was to be found on the basketball court.

"West, it's time to go," Tommy would say.

"Sure, one more game," West would reply.

Then Tommy would wait for West until he was so submerged in guilt that he could no longer make baskets. At that point, he would join Tommy for choir practice. As West would later recall, "He built character in you."[19]

Still, Tommy sensed that he was lacking something spiritually. The Baptist church was not meeting that need, so he began to sneak over to a little Pentecostal congregation, Greater Emmanuel Apostolic Church. There he discovered a much livelier service than what he had been accustomed to growing up. The people would shout, clap their hands, jump around, and embrace worship in a way he had never experienced. They also preached a message of holiness.

The Baptists were not secular in any way, but these Pentecostal people really worked at this thing called *holiness*—absolute separation in every way. They avoided movies, disapproved of television, and were careful about the clothes they wore, including jewelry and anything else that might appear to reflect the ways of the world. Later, T. D. would come to understand that although there is a place for preaching modesty and separation, it is the attitude of the heart that matters most to God, not following a set of rules. But for many years, Tommy Jakes worked hard to do the things—or not do the things—that would cause people to judge him in any way.

He found that he really enjoyed the enthusiastic services, but as time

> Tommy sensed that he was lacking something spiritually. So he began to sneak over to a little Pentecostal congregation.

went on, he also began to become receptive to the moving of the Holy Spirit in his life. He began to listen to sermons about experiencing the power of God and realized that this was the "next level" he had been searching for. In time, he received the baptism of the Holy Spirit. This experience radically changed his life at a time when most of the Baptists he knew weren't open to the charismatic movement.

As a teenager, he had no way of knowing the impact that joining this Pentecostal church would have on his life. What he didn't realize at the time was that this particular branch of the Pentecostal church believed in something called "oneness," a doctrine that would create great controversy later in his life, a controversy that still follows Jakes to this day. Nevertheless, feeling the call of God on his life as he had in the Baptist church, at the age of seventeen he accepted the call.

ON THE RUN

Tommy Jakes immediately had the feeling that he was called by God to be a preacher. He felt a sense of purpose and believed that nothing would be as fulfilling, satisfying, or meaningful as becoming a preacher. Jakes, however, was still a boy at heart and, like many boys in similar situations, he began to doubt whether anyone could really hear a word from God—so, he ran.

Tommy Jakes spent a year and half running. He had quit high school but received a high school diploma by getting his GED. He began attending West Virginia State College. One night he wandered into a local bar. It was 1975, when the drinking laws were much less stringent, and Tommy was of legal drinking age at eighteen years old. The man next to him at the bar looked at him and said, "You know, I had a dream that I saw you preaching."[20]

At that point, Tommy realized he couldn't run from God anymore, and the prodigal son returned to announce to his pastor and church family that he was going to be obedient to the call of God on his life and start preaching. Soon he preached his first sermon at Greater Emmanuel Apostolic Church. He had received no adult guidance to assist him in becoming the preacher and pastor that God wanted him to be. Although he had attended church most of his life, he did not have a strong foundation in biblical doctrine. As he fumbled through his first sermon, no one in attendance that day would have imagined that this young high school dropout would one day become one of America's most influential preachers and leaders. Everyone in the congregation certainly would have agreed that it would take a miracle for that to happen.

EARLY DAYS OF MINISTRY

I grew up in the hills of West Virginia and was a preacher
of a little tiny church. I didn't set out to be famous.
My goal was to be effective.

—T. D. Jakes[21]

Chapter Three

EARLY DAYS OF MINISTRY

A nswering the "call" to become a preacher may seem unusual to people in mainline denominations who are more accustomed to a young man or woman attending either a Bible college or seminary as part of a formal ordination process. Once the student has completed seminary training, he or she traditionally works either in a full-time capacity on staff with a large church, pastors a smaller local church, or perhaps works in a specialized field, such as counseling, youth work, or prison ministry. With experience and seasoning, the climb up the ecclesiastical career ladder begins.

This is not the way that it works in many Pentecostal churches. T. D. Jakes announced that the Lord had called him to become a preacher even though he had no seminary degree and little formal education. He had been able to obtain his GED and had enrolled at West Virginia State University for a year or so, majoring in psychology. He had worked in the music ministry at the small Baptist church of his youth but that was the extent of his apprenticeship.

As was the norm for Pentecostal preachers, Jakes was examined by a group of ministers and received a license from his denomination and thus started his career. He preached his first sermon in 1977 at Greater Emmanuel Apostolic Church at the age of nineteen. His heart was in his throat as he walked up the long aisle to the pulpit. As he turned to face the sparse congregation, he wept, overwhelmed by the fact that the calling he had received was becoming reality. He pulled forward the stand until the microphone was right in front of his mouth and clenched his hands firmly behind his back so the people wouldn't be able to see how much he was trembling. So began the ministry of the man some would eventually call America's best preacher.

SPREADING HIS WINGS

As a teenaged preacher, Jakes was somewhat of a novelty at churches where he preached. He would generally speak for youth activities or as a guest evangelist. In those early days, he preached wherever he could, including garages, porches, and storefront churches.

> Some years ago I was birthing my ministry in terms of evangelism. I was preaching in places most up-and-coming ministers would not want to go. It was not at all uncommon for me to drive hours in to some rural, secluded, 'backwoods' area to minister to a handful of people who were often financially, and in some cases mentally, deprived! I thought I was traveling to minister to the people, but in actuality God was taking me through a series of hurdles and obstacles in order to strengthen my legs for the sprints ahead.[22]

With his sharp mind and agile tongue, he soon developed a growing reputation within his association of churches, and was invited to accompany the head of the Pentecostal Association on a speaking trip throughout West Virginia. During this time, Jakes was able to perfect his style and manner in the pulpit. One of the things many of the great preachers of history know is that the best way to learn how to preach is to *preach*. In his journal, George Whitefield wrote of preaching fifteen or twenty times in a week, including six or eight times on Sundays. John Wesley wrote of speaking in the fields and barns to anyone and everyone who would listen. Obviously, it can be beneficial to take courses in the basics of outlining sermons and methods of public speaking and preaching, but there is no substitute for experience and practice.

Finally, in 1980, at the still tender age of twenty-three, Tommy Jakes started his own church, Greater Emmanuel Temple of Faith, located in a small storefront in Montgomery, West Virginia. At that time, Montgomery was a small town of about two thousand people, only around 20 percent of whom—about four hundred—were African-American. On that first Sunday, there were ten people in the pews, including Jakes's mother, Odith, and sister, Jacqueline, who had come to encourage him. Odith continued to encourage her son in the ministry until her death, while Jacqueline still serves with her brother in ministry. Five of the ten people present that morning were the family of West Womack, the young man Jakes had dragged off the basketball court years earlier. He had not forgotten the difference Jakes had made in his life.

Although he was the pastor of a small church, in his heart he was still a young man, which was apparent by the clothes he wore and the car he drove. Today, Jakes often reflects upon that car:

> Oh, man, that car was a bomb. A 1979 silver anniversary Trans Am. It had a red dashboard that lit up and a T-top and a great sound system. I couldn't drive a stick, but I faked it. Before we were married, I came to pick up my wife for a date, in that Trans Am. I blew her away. And I did funeral processions in that car.[23]

Jakes claims that he did manage to leave the t-top on whenever he conducted funerals.

A SECRET ADMIRER

As a young man Jakes was, of course, interested in the ladies, but being a young man in the ministry complicated his search for a spouse. As he preached at small churches throughout West Virginia, Jakes often noticed the young women, and they were looking at him as well. Young preachers were considered a "good catch" among mothers of eligible daughters. Jakes was no exception, given his preaching potential and the fact that he still had a good job at Union Carbide.

One Sunday, while serving as a guest preacher, he caught the eye of one of the young ladies in the church, Serita Jamison. She was taken by this tall and handsome young man whose words moved everyone in the congregation. Serita recognized the calling the Lord had on his life and this energized her even more. She wanted to attract his attention, but she didn't want to be seen as forward. However, Serita feared that if she did nothing, he would never notice her. It had to be something unexpected and clever. After much prayer, she decided to start writing Jakes secret pen pal letters.

At first, Serita would drop Jakes little encouraging notes, nothing too romantic or mushy. She included a return address but dared not reveal her identity. She later admitted that she feared he was so spiritual that "it wouldn't behoove me to come at him in a carnal light."[24] She wrote him notes of encouragement as he was going through the process of learning to preach and reach out to people. She was taking a big chance and did not know if she would ever get any response from the notes. A week or so after the first note, she received a response from him and they began a correspondence similar to overseas pen pals. Each note she received from him opened the door to a possible relationship and captured a little more of her heart. It wasn't long before she was dying to reveal her identity. But having started out as a secret pen pal, Serita was unsure of how Jakes might respond once she revealed herself to be the letter writer. If she did not reveal herself, of course, there was no chance she would ever be able to develop a relationship with him. Finally, she took the chance and wrote to tell him who she was and how and where she had seen him the first time.

> With his sharp mind and agile tongue, Jakes soon developed a growing reputation within his association of churches.

THE JOURNEY OF T. D. JAKES

A few days after her note of confession, Serita went to church, where it was announced that the following Sunday there would be a special guest speaker—T. D. Jakes! He would not only be speaking on Sunday, but he would also be holding a revival for an entire week. Serita was both excited and terrified at the same time. She was not sure what do when he came—whether she should go up and speak to him or if she should wait for him to seek her out. It seemed more ladylike to wait for him to make a move, but there was always the chance that he might not—and she couldn't bear that! Jakes had sent no response to Serita's note. She didn't know if he was ready to take their secret relationship to a public level or not.

Serita decided to attend the service but slip out and go home as soon as it was over. When the moment came and she was slipping out of the church, her pastor's wife called out to her. She motioned for Serita to come up front and join them. Put on the spot and not wanting to disappoint her pastor's wife, Serita crept forward, looking around to see if she could see Jakes. As soon as she reached the front, Tommy Jakes himself was walking over in their direction. The pastor's wife proceeded to do the introductions. Serita was thrilled and frightened at the same time. Jakes smiled and shook her hand. When her name was mentioned, his eyes lit up with recognition, and he asked, "Do you know where a bachelor can get a good home-cooked meal?"

Serita was so stunned that she didn't know what to say. She blurted back, "I'll ask my mother." Immediately, she wanted to find a hole and crawl inside it to hide. Finally, Tommy Jakes had spoken to her and she had responded like a little schoolgirl.

Jakes simply nodded his head and continued the conversation. His eyes were so filled with her that his ears did not really care what she said. The fact that he had heard her voice for the first time was enough for him. He asked her how she had enjoyed the service, about the church, and about herself. He asked her anything and everything that came into his head.

Serita did not miss a single service of the revival, and Jakes did not miss any opportunity to speak to her—before and after the service. During the week, Jakes did enjoy one of Serita's mother's home-cooked meals. It was the first of many meals he would eat there.

This was the beginning of a courtship that would continue for several months. Their notes gave way to long phone calls, which then gave way to dating and courtship whenever and wherever the opportunity presented itself. Jakes was working the swing shift at Union Carbide, which meant that he would go to work in the middle of the afternoon and get off at midnight. He would come home from work in the middle of the night and call Serita, waking her up from a deep sleep, but that was unimportant to her. Jakes would pour out his heart to her. He would tell her his hopes and dreams, what he felt the Lord had in store for him, and of the call that God had on his life. He would also tell her of his troubles and of his doubts that he would ever become a full-time pastor. Serita listened, knowing that he was tired and that he had a tendency to feel overwhelmed and depressed about his problems. As best she could, Serita would encourage Jakes and counsel him not to overreact. She often reminded him that things would look different after a good night's rest.

> Young preachers were considered a "good catch" among mothers of eligible daughters. Jakes was no exception.

As the relationship grew, their love for each other became strong. When it seemed obvious that marriage was in their future, he told his friend, "I'm going to marry that girl." His friend replied, "How do you know?" Tommy simply said, "I just know."

Despite his love for Serita, Jakes was having a hard time getting to the proposal. Today, it seems impossible to imagine Thomas Dexter Jakes having a hard time getting words out, but he did. Finally, he got close enough to getting the words out that they both needed to hear: "I'm assuming you'll marry me." Perhaps not the height of romantic expression, but it was enough for Serita, who said yes.

T. D. would later describe how he knew that Serita was the one God had for him.

> I remember one date and when I got ready to go, she started crying. I said, "Oh, girl, I'll be back. What are you crying for?" She said, "I'm okay. I'm just going to miss you." And I believed her…I trusted her and out of that trust came love for her. And I still trust and love her today.[25]

DOING WHATEVER IT TAKES

In 1981, a little more than six months after their courtship began, Thomas Dexter Jakes and Serita Jamison were united in marriage. Serita knew she was assuming the role of pastor's wife and took to it enthusiastically. Jakes would work at the chemical plant by day and preach anywhere he could by night. He worked hard to keep food on his new family's table. In 1982, Serita gave birth to twin sons, Jermaine and Jamar. By now, the family was truly living from paycheck to paycheck, but it was Jakes's hope to save enough money to buy a home. He had seen his father set this goal and achieve it, and he was determined to do the same for his family. He also set a goal to buy a second suit so he wouldn't have to preach in the same one every Sunday.

When he traveled, Jakes, now known as T. D. instead of Tommy, preached to humble people in humble sanctuaries. In these small, clapboard halls, the summertime air-conditioning was often a hand fan with Martin Luther King's picture on one side and an advertisement for the local funeral home on the other. He was blessed if there was a microphone to save wear and tear on his voice. The "love offering" sometimes consisted of some fried chicken and cornbread or a couple of pound cakes and a few jars of jelly.

Early Days of Ministry

At his own church, Jakes, despite limited musical ability, would often play the piano his mother had bought him for Christmas many years earlier, while Serita was the praise and worship leader. Later, one of his friends, today an associate pastor at The Potter's House, would say, "When I came into the church, he'd play piano and sing and then go up and preach."[26] The "church bus" was the Jakes family car. After church, T. D. would go home with his growing family and as many people as he could squeeze into his car, whose gas gauge was usually hovering around the empty mark. T. D. was a hard worker, doing everything he could to make his ministry a success. That success did not come quickly or easily.

It was during these early and lean days that T. D. Jakes honed and perfected his preaching skills. He would preach to a handful of people and rows of empty pews until he was tired and sweaty. As he studied the Word in preparation for his messages week after week, he memorized many of the Bible verses that he recites in messages today. Jakes paid his preaching dues in ways that many preachers at megachurches throughout America never have—all while holding down a full-time position at Union Carbide.

TIMES OF ADVERSITY

A turning point came in 1982 when Jakes was laid off from his job at Union Carbide. There was not a lot of opportunity in West Virginia, especially for an African-American man without a college education. Add to that his desire to pastor a church, and the job prospects were not strong. T. D. would later describe the situation.

> We were laid off and found ourselves going from what I thought was an adequate income to no income at all and entered into a very depressed economic desert.[27]

Serita has also remarked on that time in their lives.

The unemployment [money] ran out. And he was digging ditches with his brother to lay gas lines and preaching revivals to subsidize our income. I worked as a DJ at a Christian radio station at night, but little did I realize that it was deflating his masculine instinct to want to take care of the family.[28]

Despite being one of the economically poorest periods of their lives, Jakes described it as one of the richest times for his personal growth.

We lost everything. And it was a real fight to get back up. I'm glad it happened, from the standpoint that I can relate to extremely poor people. I was literally cutting grass and digging ditches, trying to get diapers for my kids. So when I go into a home of somebody who doesn't have lights on, I've been there. I know what it is to get government milk.[29]

During this time, Jakes determined in his heart never to become dependent on a single source of income. He knew full well that God was the source of his sustenance, but he also knew that God had gifted him in several areas and that he should use every gift that God had given him to support his family. In addition, over the course of many years, Jakes earned bachelor's, master's, and doctoral degrees, all by correspondence from Friends International Christian University. His education did not always come in conventional times or methods, but T. D. Jakes stayed true to the early training of his mother and has always been a lifelong learner.

These were difficult years for the Jakes family. Many nights, T. D. would toss and turn, praying and worrying about how he was going to provide for his growing family. He and Serita would collect pop bottles and redeem them for the deposit to help with grocery money. There were tough decisions about whether to pay the light bill or buy food. The frustration often led Jakes to cry out, "Where are You, Lord?" All around him, it seemed that people were living in abundance, yet he and his family were struggling. His car was in such bad shape that one Sunday when there were guests at church, one of the deacons volunteered to hide his car behind the church building so no one would see it. Other times, the car would break down entirely, and he would have to thumb a ride to church so he could preach, leaving his family at home. Serita would often boil water and pour it into the tub so they could have hot baths. The gas was off much of the time, and the lights some of the time. There were candlelight dinners that were neither romantic nor optional. T. D. and Serita Jakes were trying to make the best of a very difficult situation. They often ate with Serita's parents so the children could be well fed. Jakes had always been a hard worker and he had assumed he would always be able to work and provide well for his family. Being in financial straits was not the vision he'd had for his family when he'd asked Serita to marry him.

> **Jakes determined in his heart never to become dependent on a single source of income.**

On one occasion when his car had broken down again, Jakes had to take a bus downtown in an attempt to convince the electric company to keep the lights on, even though he had no money to give them. Despite his promise to pay as soon as he could, the young lady at the utility company was unmoved and ordered the lights turned off. Jakes was crushed by her seemingly cruel and unmerciful response. Not only had he been laid off from his job, and not only was his church unable to pay his salary, but the electric company had just turned his lights off.

As he shuffled out the door of the electric company, Jakes recalls that the devil began to speak to him.

> You're going to be homeless. You will be pushing a go-cart. You and Serita and the boys are going to be on the street and eating out of trashcans![30]

T. D. burst into tears. He had promised Serita that he would take care of her and the boys, but now they had nothing. Seeing his distress, some people walking on the street asked if he was all right or if they could do anything to help him. Yet, in the midst of this total meltdown, God apparently said nothing to him. The doors of heaven seemed to be slammed shut.

When he finally settled down, the Lord seemed to say to him, "I will not suffer thy foot to be moved!" (See Psalm 121:3.)

"What did You say?" Jakes replied.

The Lord repeated, "I will not suffer thy foot to be moved."

FULL-TIME MINISTRY

Through those nine words, God began to assure Jakes that even in the midst of his troubles, He had not forsaken him and would lead him to a better place. The vision the devil had suggested was not from God but from the enemy of God—and it was a lie. This was not a time of suffering, but a time of training in the Lord.[31]

With this gentle encouragement from God, Jakes decided to view the loss of a job as an opportunity to go full-time in the ministry. It wasn't his choice to make the transition, but he began to look for a new facility that would hold his growing church. He located a vacant, run-down theater in Smithers, West Virginia, a small town of about a thousand people located on the outskirts of Montgomery, yet close enough to the old location that people could easily drive there. To most people who passed by, it was not much to see, just an old, smelly movie theater with large sections of the roof torn off. Inside, rotted seat cushions were scattered about. T. D. even fell through the floor the first time he walked in the building. Yet Serita recalls that in T. D.'s eyes, this was a theater that could become a great cathedral. In the midst of the sticky, disintegrating floor and trash, Jakes could envision a choir loft, pews, and Sunday school rooms. He knew great things were ahead for him if he would just remain faithful. Serita could not see everything her husband saw, but she had faith in God and in her husband, and she stood and worked beside him in turning that nightmare into a dream.[32]

T. D. and Serita worked hard on their new church home, painting and cleaning the place so it would look its best for the grand opening. It seemed as though they were working around the clock to do everything that needed to be done. They would spend some time ministering to the needs of the congregation and the rest of their time doing the physical work of improving the new facility.

When the day finally came for the first service in their new church home, Jakes held his Bible with hands that bled from hours of holding a paintbrush and roller. Only Serita knew that he was standing behind the pulpit in house slippers because his swollen feet would not fit into his shoes. She also knew that he was standing in his only suit, cleaned and pressed for the occasion. Throughout that first service, she prayed that her husband would not collapse from exhaustion before it was over. The Lord, however, rewarded their hard work as their first Sunday in the new building was so packed that there weren't enough chairs for all of the people.

> When the day finally came for the first service in their new church home, Jakes held his Bible with hands that bled from hours of holding a paintbrush and roller.

T. D. and Serita did whatever it took to make the ministry work. He played piano. He used his car, when it was running, to pick up as many people for services as he could. He taught the Sunday school classes and often did the janitorial work and the upkeep on the building. When offerings were low, he would raise funds to pay the rent on the church, and the deacons would pay the light bill.

It was at this time that Jakes began a media ministry. He started a radio show called *The Master's Plan*. This helped to get word out about the church and allowed people to hear his words of encouragement, which brought more and more people into the church. After a few months, the church outgrew its little movie theater and moved into larger facilities at a local shopping mall.

Jakes's preaching began to stand out to those in the community who visited the church as well as those who heard him on the radio. Word spread as he gained a growing reputation as a strong preacher of the Word of God. His radio show continued for about three years, until 1985.

Holloway Gray, now his personal assistant, first went to hear him preach in the early 1980s.

> When someone is good, you kind of hear about him....The Spirit of the Lord just moved so mightily in the church that particular Sunday, and a friend of mine said, "Well, you know, this is normal for us." And I told my wife—got back in the car—I said, "Ahh, I don't believe that." You just can't believe church is that great every Sunday.[33]

No matter what it was that attracted people to the church, it was the preaching that kept them coming back.

TRUSTING GOD

Yet at this time of great growth in the church, adversity revisited T. D. Jakes and his family. One day, as a speeding jeep passed the Jakes's van, it attempted a hairpin turn too fast and bumped the van, which crashed and collapsed like a tin can. Inside were T. D., Serita, Serita's mother, and the twins. They weren't wearing seatbelts. It was a time when most states did not mandate seatbelt use. As the accident occurred, T. D. hit the windshield while his mother-in-law tried to protect the children in the back seat with her own body. Afterward, T. D. climbed out of his side of the car with blood flowing from a wound on his head. Serita tried to move but found she couldn't. She looked down to see what the problem was and saw a bone protruding from her skin. Her leg was broken, and her heel was crushed. They waited for the paramedics to arrive, not fully aware of the severity of her injuries.

At the hospital, the seriousness of the damage became apparent. After some tests, the doctors said that Serita's heel was so badly crushed that she might never walk normally again. Over the next several days, weeks, and months, this was their constant pronouncement. Each time she saw a doctor, the physician warned her not to get her hopes up. Regardless of how well she thought she was doing, she was told that her chances were small.

T. D. Jakes was a man doing his best to serve the Lord, working a full-time job while leading a church. When he'd lost his job and the family economy had been devastated, he'd continued to trust in God. Now, he'd been involved in an accident, not through any fault of his own, and he'd lost his car and very likely his wife's health in an instant. This kind of turn of events might very well have destroyed or discouraged most men. Many people would have grown angry, blamed God, or even decided that there must not be a God. T. D. simply did what he had always done. He kept on going.

Serita left the hospital to continue her recovery at home. She believed in the promises of the Word of God, and she lived on this particular promise:

God, who gives life to the dead and calls those things which do not exist as though they did. (Romans 4:17)

Even though the doctors had insisted that she would forever be crippled, Serita trusted that God would bring wholeness and healing to her body. She was unable to place even the smallest amount of weight on her foot, but managed to get around on crutches, with a shoe on one foot and a cast on the other.

After some time, the doctor replaced the cast with a brace. Serita was told that she would probably have to wear the brace for the rest of her life. Once again, she was assaulted with words of discouragement, words that lacked any sort of hope. Because of this devastating diagnosis, she lay on her bed and wept bitter tears, afraid that her husband would no longer find her attractive. One day, as she was moving around the bedroom dragging her lame foot behind her, T. D. silently stepped up behind her and picked her up in his arms. He told her that he loved her and that if she never walked again, he would be honored to push her around in a wheelchair. He reminded her that not a day went by that he did not thank God for giving him such a wife.[34]

Tenderly, T. D. cared for his wife in every way that he could. She would hang her head over the couch as he washed her hair with a pail of water. Over the next few months, Serita pushed herself to walk again. Her healing was not instantaneous, but this did not stop her from maintaining her faith.

T. D. encouraged her with every step. He would not let her give up. He would stand a few feet from her and hold his hands out to support her. First, she was able to walk from the bed to the bathroom, then from the bedroom to the dining room and living room. Finally, she was able to walk out of her house and go back to church again. As her walking improved, her shoes began to change as well. She started with sneakers, moved to flat shoes, then to small heels, and finally back to the pumps that she had worn before the accident. She had finally completely recovered her health. In spite of the doctors' ominous decrees, Serita Jakes was walking once again.

The Jakeses expanded their family with the births of two daughters a year apart. Cora was born in 1987 and Sarah in 1988. When Cora was about three months old, she became ill. She had been listless and colicky, crying and obviously not feeling well. T. D. and Serita thought it was a typical childhood illness. By this time, Serita was pregnant once again with Sarah and had been up with Cora for a couple of nights in a row, so T. D. thought it best if he took Cora to the doctor to be examined and diagnosed so Serita could stay home and rest.

When the doctor examined Cora, he told T. D. that her condition was quite serious and that she should be hospitalized immediately. Cora was severely dehydrated and had a virus the doctor could not identify without additional tests that could be performed only in a hospital. In addition, she needed to be hydrated as quickly as possible before the lack of water began to severely impact parts of her body.

This was not the word that T. D. had expected to hear. He was in shock that this little girl, his only daughter, was so ill that she needed serious medical attention. After he left the doctor's office, he stopped at his mother's house so she could accompany them to the hospital. Despite the fact that he did not want

> T. D. lamented to his mother that he would far prefer to bear this burden himself than have his child experience it. Odith understood.

his mother to realize the fear he had in his heart, Jakes found that he could not keep this dreadful information to himself. He told his mother that he could not bear the thought of this child, whom he loved, in a hospital connected to all those tubes and wires. Cora was only a baby and wouldn't understand why all this was happening. He lamented that he would far prefer to bear this burden himself than have his child experience it.

Odith empathized because she felt the same way. She would gladly have taken the place of her children when they were in pain. As they drove to the hospital, T. D. began to understand the depth of a father's love. He would often use this experience in later years to communicate to his congregation the depth of God's love.[35]

Before heading to the hospital, T. D. and Odith stopped at home to tell Serita of the doctor's conclusion and instructions. As he walked up to his front door, Jakes vowed to be the brave, strong husband—the man of God, full of faith. Once inside, all his plans fell apart and he instead blurted out the news to his wife. The twins scampered upstairs at the sight of the emotional outburst as their parents wept and held on to each other for comfort while Odith held the sick baby. Despite the depths of his fear and worry, T. D. realized at that moment that Cora would be just fine. He knew that he had to place his daughter in the arms of the Lord believing that her fate was assured. With this peace in his heart, Jakes took Cora to the hospital, where she made a complete recovery, and where T. D. learned another lesson in faith.

OUT OF TESTING, INTO BLESSING

It would be fifteen years from the time that Tommy Jakes preached his first sermon in 1977 to the time that the world began to hear about T. D. Jakes in 1992. During those years, T. D. married, experienced the difficulty and humiliation of struggling to put food on the table and a roof over the heads of his family members, and started a small storefront church where he honed his preaching and leadership abilities. T. D. also learned about building a church from the ground up, working without a staff or large budget. He developed compassion for people as he visited them in the hospitals, comforted them when they lost family members, and helped them as they struggled to provide the daily needs of their children. He experienced firsthand the issues that burdened their lives. He felt their pain and knew the guilt and worries that they carried with them everyday. The Lord created within him a heart for evangelism as he reached out to everyone in his community while building his church. The Lord created within him a heart of compassion as he loved people and saw their needs. These were the years of trial and hardship where T. D. Jakes was being developed by God to become the man he was meant to be.

For fifteen years, T. D. Jakes seemed to come up short more often than he was able to succeed. He remained faithful through struggles and hardship, testing and trials. At the end of this time, the blessings of God would begin to appear. Little did Jakes realize that through these blessings, many thousands and perhaps millions of others would be blessed as well.

Woman, Thou Art Loosed!

People need to know that those who've been abused,
who've been molested, who've been in jail, who've been
ostracized, criticized, who've had a baby by Mary over here
and another one by Isabel over there, can come to Christ, need
not hide who they were, can be rehabilitated, can become
productive—and that God has grace to receive them.

—T. D. Jakes[36]

Chapter Four

WOMAN, THOU ART LOOSED!

In the late 1980s and early 90s, a rare thing began to occur in T. D. Jakes's ministry, especially for a rural state like West Virginia: white people began to attend his church. Most church experts lament the fact that ten o'clock on Sunday mornings is the most segregated hour of the week in America. It is unusual to see African-Americans worshipping side by side with whites, or Hispanics for that matter. Although this does occur at some high profile megachurches today, for white people to attend a small church where the majority of the congregation is African-American was unheard of at that time. Nevertheless, whites and Hispanics began to hear that God was doing something at Jakes's church and that everyone was welcome to be a part of the experience.

One of the first white men to attend and later become a member described his reasons for leaving his all-white church in favor of a more diverse congregation:

> I am just tired of being around people who dress like me, look like me, and think like me. My life is boring. I want to see the many facets of God and life. I appreciate what I have, and those of my own status, race, and place. But I am tired of living in a microcosm, a carefully controlled environment that doesn't allow me the opportunity for real meaningful exchange.[37]

MOVING TO THE CITY

While at the converted theater in Smithers, Greater Emmanuel Temple of Faith grew from about one hundred to over three hundred members, and its pastor, T. D. Jakes, was building a strong and growing reputation around West Virginia. Before long, Bishop Sherman Watkins, founder of Higher Ground Always Abounding Assembly and Jakes's ordaining bishop, encouraged T. D. to start a church in the Charleston area. Watkins's association of some two hundred churches needed an anchor church and a strong presence in Charleston, the capital of West Virginia and the most prominent city in the state. Bishop Watkins also realized that T. D. Jakes had a special anointing on his life and needed a bigger platform for his ministry.

> Whites and Hispanics began to hear that God was doing something at Jakes's church and that everyone was welcome to be a part of the experience.

Thus, in 1990, T. D., Serita, and their family moved to South Charleston, West Virginia. This move was undoubtedly a tough decision. Because Charleston is a good distance from Montgomery and Smithers, Jakes knew that it would mean starting over. Most pastors who build a three-hundred-member church from scratch are then ready to move on to a bigger and more prestigious congregation. Very few, especially those with families, would relish the idea of building a church from scratch all over again. As it turned out, a few from Smithers followed Jakes to Charleston, but most balked at the prospect of driving a half hour to and from church. At his first service in South Charleston, Jakes had about forty people, but it wasn't long before the congregation began to grow and thrive. Soon, people were driving from all around the Charleston area to attend the services.

Moving to Charleston was a bold step for Jakes for another reason as well: he was leaving the comfort zone of a small, rural, Appalachian town and venturing into what was, by comparison, the big city. There were many challenges in planting the new church. Charleston was a city of over a hundred thousand people but had a minority community of less than 10 percent. In order to have a major impact on this new community, Jakes's church would have to be a diverse congregation.

In 1991, a much larger church in Washington, D.C., recognized the calling on T. D.'s life and asked him to become their pastor. Jakes was tempted. It was a bigger venue and, because of its prominence and location in the nation's capital, Jakes knew that if he moved there, many more opportunities would present themselves. He would consider such a move, however, only if it were the will of the Lord. After much prayer, Jakes declined the invitation because he felt it was important to remain in West Virginia.

The church moved once again in 1993 to a former bank building in Cross Lanes, West Virginia, a suburb of Charleston. The new location provided enough space to accommodate hundreds of worshippers. They cleared the space where the teller windows and offices were and created a nice sanctuary with a seating capacity of five hundred. It looked more like a multipurpose room with a low ceiling than a church. It was very functional but not particularly impressive to guests. On the outside, the building still looked like a bank. Perhaps the most unusual feature in the new building was the large shower in the pastor's office. One has only to observe the amount of perspiration pouring off Jakes's face during a message to understand the absolute necessity of such an amenity. Having gone through the relocation process more than once by then, Jakes was well aware of the importance of the resale value of a property. Thus, nothing was done to the building that might decrease any value for business purposes in the future.

Woman, Thou Art Loosed!

RESPONDING TO THE NEED

Having started his ministry in a rural community, Jakes had a particular concern and appreciation for pastors in rural areas. Wanting to share what he had learned since his days in the storefront church, Jakes instituted an annual conference called Back to the Bible. The conference has continued in some form without interruption wherever and whenever the church moved. By the early 1990s, it was attracting thousands of pastors from some twenty states, as well as Canada and Africa. At the same time, Jakes became a popular speaker at other church conferences, further enhancing his reputation and influence.

Jakes also had a particular compassion and understanding for the women in his congregation. Perhaps this was due to the influence of his mother, or perhaps it was simply due to the fact that his church, like many small churches, had an abundance of women in the pews. As Jakes pastored and counseled these women, he quickly realized that he was hearing the same sad stories over and over. His heart ached for these women, and he wanted to do something that would give them the support and courage they needed to break the cycles of abuse, addiction, poverty, single parenting, and self-hatred. Too often, he would minister to these women only to see their daughters in the same circumstances a few years later. He knew that if nothing changed, eventually he would witness a third generation of women suffering from the same problems. Something had to be done to help these ladies experience the life-changing love of God.

Jakes also recognized the mixed message that many churches, and many Pentecostal churches, in particular, sent to women. He had seen men who had fathered a child or two out of wedlock go to the altar and repent and be welcomed back into the church with open arms. If they remained faithful after their confession, many of these men became deacons or elders in the church. When a woman had a child or two out of wedlock, however, she was often treated differently, viewed by many as a "tramp" or a woman of loose morals and forced to become an outcast. In many cases, no matter how many times she repented, she was still viewed as suspect and not to be trusted. Even if she was accepted back into the church, she rarely was able to regain the same respect that a man could. In a seminar years later, Jakes told a group of women, "The churches only want you when you are pasteurized, homogenized, milksame Christian women. But some church is going to have to go out on a limb and say, 'I love you anyway. You have a slit in your skirt three feet long, but I love you.'"[38]

In general, women were encouraged to fill the pews and volunteer for everything that needed to be done in the church. They could sing in the choir, teach Sunday school, clean the facility, or prepare the potluck dinners, but if a woman felt the call of God to preach, the pulpit was not open to her. They were often told that man fell from grace because of a woman.

In 1992, Jakes began to prepare a Sunday school lesson for a class of forty women in his church. He sought the Lord's wisdom on how to address these recurring situations. Through all those counseling sessions with hurting women, some things had become evident to him.

> Many of them had deep scars and secret issues that they were unable to really work through and generally thought that they were the only ones who had ever gone through anything that horrendous. If they could meet each other and find out that they were not alone, that would be a great way to minister to them. And my job as a pastor was to provide biblical answers to sociological ills.[39]

Jakes also prayed about the confessions he had heard from many of the women he and Serita had counseled.

> I had been counseling as a pastor and I noticed there was a common thread in the secrets of many women who came in for help. I thought, *Why keep doing this individually? Why not bring everyone together and just have a mass session?*[40]

Woman, Thou Art Loosed!

When the Lord spoke to him and led him to fill this need, he feared that some people would think he was crazy. You just didn't talk about these subjects in church, especially if you were a man. They were too personal, too intimate, and some might become offended and ostracize him.

When he presented the lesson, the ladies in the class were deeply touched. While preparing the material, Jakes had assumed he could cover all of it in one class period. As is the case with many pastors, however, he had so much to say on his subject that it had to be carried over another week. The women from that first class brought their friends and neighbors to the next one. Some of these women attended other churches, but what Jakes was teaching was so unique that it touched something within them. At that point, Jakes thought, *Let's go another week; I'm really on a roll.*

The class *rolled on* through a second week and then a third. By the end of the month, there were so many women attending that they had to stand in the hall outside the classroom trying to hear lessons that didn't even have a name at that point.

Jakes's sister, Jacqueline, attended those classes and remembers the situation clearly.

> He had been a pastor for a while by then, so he had a lot of broken women coming to him, sharing intimate things about what was happening to them. He began to minister to them one on one. Then he taught the Sunday school class. It was so good that we said, "Do it again." And this went on for six weeks and women began to come from their church to his Sunday school class so they could hear the teaching.[41]

Indeed, word was traveling outside the walls of his church that there was a teaching that touched and uplifted women who found themselves in difficult situations.

Eventually, Jakes found a name for these lessons: "Woman, Thou Art Loosed!" It came from a passage in Scripture about a woman who had been crippled for eighteen years to the point that she could not stand upright. She went to Jesus while He was teaching in the synagogue on the Sabbath. *"When Jesus saw her, he called her to him, and said unto her, Woman, thou art loosed from thine infirmity"* (Luke 13:12 KJV). The religious people of the time were not happy because Jesus healed the woman on the Sabbath. Jesus, it seemed, saw the woman's need as more important than social customs or the need to obey man's interpretation of God's law. Through His love and compassion, Jesus reached out and changed the woman's life. Jakes expanded on this theme, telling the women that Jesus had compassion upon them, as well, and wanted to "loose" them from the terrible burdens they were carrying.

> You just didn't talk about these subjects in church, especially if you were a man. They were too personal, too intimate, and some might become offended.

It is doubtful that Jakes had the slightest inkling that these lessons would set into motion something that would change his life forever and influence the lives of millions of women throughout the United States and many parts of the world. For the first time, many of these women began to realize that the Lord desired to touch them and make them whole. It did not matter how long they had suffered or how severe their problems were. Jesus loved them despite their past circumstances and did not see them as "damaged goods" but as people of value for whom He was willing to die.

For a male church leader, Jakes showed an amazing sensitivity to the plight of women. He told them that not all of the hardship they were experiencing was their fault. He reminded them that they had a heavenly Father who loved them and didn't wish to condemn them but heal them. He taught them that the Lord wanted to lead them down a path that would take them from the depths of despair to the highest heavenly realm. He assured them that their lives were not set in stone and that God had a divine plan for them if they were able to receive it by faith. He explained that the pain of their past could not compare to the marvelous things ahead of them if they would just open their hearts and accept God's plan for their lives.

This was subject matter and truth that much of the Christian church tended to ignore. Too often, because of the somewhat sensitive nature of these issues, they were dealt with indirectly or swept under the rug. After all, most church leaders were *men* who generally misunderstood or were completely insensitive to issues of sex, abuse, and the inequality of gender roles.

T. D. Jakes hit these issues head-on and presented an entirely different perspective on them. He cast the spotlight on many of the serious problems plaguing the African-American community, as well as much of American society and the world. He dealt with issues of infidelity and premarital sex. Many Christians act as if the relational problems people face today are unique to modern society, but obviously this is not so. The woman at the well in John 4 had been married five times and was living with someone who was not her husband. These issues have been problems for thousands of years. Jakes believed that if people knew that these problems had been around for that long, and that others had found healing, then maybe they'd begin to believe that there *was* a solution for them, too.

Jakes also dealt with the delicate topics of abuse and molestation, which have become such serious issues in the lives of so many people. This is partly due to the rise in the divorce rate. In direct terms, when a woman is divorced and brings a new man into the family who is not biologically related to her children, and if he has no integrity or moral values, he may choose to take advantage of those children sexually. As horrible as this is, it is a sad reality for many children today.

Because many of these children are in need of a male role model, they build a degree of trust with these new men in their lives. When that trust is broken, however, it creates pain and scarring that can last a lifetime. Today, it is estimated that there are millions of men and women who were victims of abuse as children. As Jakes brought this problem out of the closet and into the open where it could be dealt with, many women, who thought they were the only ones saddled with this pain, began to discover that they were not alone. Not only did Jesus Christ love them and want to make them whole, but also there were many others who had experienced the same thing and needed healing as well.

> When a child's trust is broken, it creates pain and scarring that can last a lifetime. Today, it is estimated that there are millions of men and women who were victims of abuse as children.

Jakes also dealt with the reality of being single in a world where a woman often isn't viewed as whole until she is married, especially in the church. He used the words of the apostle Paul to assure women that remaining single was acceptable in God's eyes. "*Now to the unmarried and the widows I say: It is good for them to stay unmarried, as I am*" (1 Corinthians 7:8 NIV). He encouraged women to focus on their relationship with the Lord instead of desperately trying to find a husband.

Many of the women in those Sunday school classes were in marriages that were "unequally yoked"—that is, their husbands were not Christians. Well-meaning believers would use Scripture to warn them, "*Do not be unequally yoked together with unbelievers. For what fellowship has righteousness with lawlessness? And what communion has light with darkness?"* (2 Corinthians 6:14). These women were unsure of their responsibility to God concerning the spiritual conditions of their husbands. They didn't know if they should be nagging their husbands to go to church or secretly praying for them without saying anything. This confusion caused them to be incredibly divided in their hearts, as well as ashamed and guilt-ridden by the disappointment of other Christians—not to mention the fact that it was hard on their marriages as well.

Divorce was another issue Jakes addressed. This problem continues to be a sticky topic in the church. Many people, both men and women, are so bound by their pasts that they cannot reach the potential God has for them in the here and now. Many churches forbid those who have been divorced from serving in any leadership capacity within the church. They see divorced people as "damaged goods" or as "second-class citizens." Because of this, it is easy for some people to feel that God might view divorce as an unforgivable sin. Jakes reminded the women of the Samaritan woman at the well who had been married several times. Jesus did not hold it against her. Instead, He offered her forgiveness, healing, and eternal life. (See John 4.)

Jakes also dealt with how attitudes impact our lives. Because of traumatic experiences, abused children can hold on to certain attitudes that affect the choices they make throughout the rest of their lives. Jakes taught that we can control our attitudes instead of letting our attitudes control us. A good attitude can ensure success, but a bad attitude can ensure failure. We can rest assured that God will carry us and both protect and provide for us if we will allow Him to do so. This does not mean that every situation will be good, but that the Lord will use it for our good. We must allow God rather than our circumstances to determine our attitudes.

The emotional impact of these Sunday school classes cannot be overstated. Soon word of mouth about the classes spread far beyond the borders of West Virginia. Without any sophisticated marketing or television campaign, the women simply appeared, first by the hundreds and then by the thousands.

Jakes remembers, "I later called a friend of mine—the now deceased Reverend Archie Dennis—and said to him, 'I am teaching this class for women and it is growing in leaps and bounds.' He said, 'Why don't you come to Pittsburgh?'"[42]

Thus, a three-day Pittsburgh conference at a local church was organized. Tickets were sold for twenty dollars each and the requests began to flood in. It soon became obvious that the church would not be able to hold that many people, so they moved the conference to a local hotel ballroom. When Jakes arrived for the conference, to his amazement, thirteen hundred women had registered. Many of them did not even attend church. This was becoming an evangelistic outreach greater than he ever could have imagined. He was a little nervous because he had never before spoken to a group this large, but he was certain the Lord had given him the right message for the right time.

The conference went off without a hitch and, once again, the women were deeply touched. One of them, Barbara Tucker, spoke about that Pittsburgh conference, saying, "What he said just made so much sense. Women were weeping and shouting."[43] She shed a few tears of her own and left him with some prayer requests. According to Tucker, each of her prayer requests, from recovering a loved one from prison to rebuilding her marriage, was eventually answered.

Writing a Best Seller

The messages he gave at the conference struck such a chord with so many women that Jakes was convinced that he needed to turn them into a book. Over the next weeks and months, he shaped the lessons into a manuscript and submitted it to a publisher, who promptly rejected it. He then submitted it to another publisher, and then another, and then another. In 1993, with no company willing to publish the book, T. D. and Serita decided to take what little money they had saved for a down payment on a new home and publish the book themselves. As Jakes later said, "It was an investment, and a very frightening one, because it took every penny that I had to get it out there. I got out about 5,000 copies, emptied our bank account, and it sold out in about two weeks."[44] Eventually, the book, *Woman, Thou Art Loosed!* was published through Destiny Image Publishers. Jakes dedicated the book to his late father and mother, as well as to Serita.

The book initially came out in paperback and sold for ten dollars. *Woman, Thou Art Loosed!* went to the top of the nonfiction Christian book sales list almost immediately. This was the beginning of a major shift in the lives of T. D. and Serita. They could not have imagined the doors the book would open and the changes their lives would experience over the next four years. For the very first time in over a decade, instead of scraping money together to live month-to-month, the Jakes family was paying its bills on time routinely. The book remains the most successful one that Jakes has ever written. Even as it was first published, however, Jakes could not have dreamed that it would sell millions of copies and later be adapted into a stage play and hit movie.

JAKES IS "DISCOVERED"

In the early 1990s, the Azusa Street Conference was held annually. It attracted thousands of pastors and lay people from the charismatic and Pentecostal movements, both black and white, from across the United States and other parts of the world. It had begun in 1988 and was hosted by Bishop Carlton Pearson, who at the time was the pastor of Higher Dimension Family Church in Tulsa, Oklahoma. Pearson held the conference on the campus of Oral Roberts University at the school's athletic arena, the Mabee Center. Because the list of speakers was always a "who's who" of pastors and evangelists in the charismatic movement, attendees often planned their summer vacations around the event. Portions of the conference were often televised nationally on the Trinity Broadcasting Network. Prominent Christian leaders were always eager to step into the spotlight that the Azusa Conference provided.

In 1992, a year before the release of *Woman, Thou Art Loosed!* T. D. and Serita scraped together the funds to attend the conference for the first time. They drove and arranged to stay with friends along the way because they could not afford a plane ticket or the cost of a hotel room. Jakes was virtually unknown to everyone there. A few acquaintances of his attended, but Jakes saw this as a great opportunity to meet people and establish contacts that would be helpful in the future. Sitting high up in the arena, Jakes absorbed everything around him and was able to see a vision of what was possible in ministry.

One of Jakes's few friends at the conference introduced him to Pearson and encouraged the conference host to listen to some of T. D.'s sermon tapes. After the conference, Pearson did indeed listen to the tapes and was impressed by what he heard. It didn't hurt that, soon after the conference, Jakes's conferences and book were starting to create quite a buzz. Pearson invited Jakes to speak at the Azusa Pastor's Conference at Higher Dimension Family Church. It was not the national conference, but it was still a major invitation and an excellent opportunity to meet people and to be introduced to a wider audience.

T. D. was one of three speakers at the conference, and he gave a message on Thursday night called "Behind Closed Doors." During one section of the sermon, Jakes spoke dramatically of Christ showing His wounds to the apostles behind closed doors in the house where they had gathered. The message made a big impression on those who attended, but its influence reached far beyond the walls of that conference.

Pearson's television show on TBN showed a seven-minute video clip from each of the three sermons at the conference. When the program aired, Paul Crouch, president of TBN, was coming home from a long trip abroad. At that time, he was in the midst of writing his autobiography, *I Had No Father but God,* and he was struggling with whether or not to share some rather difficult details from his life. He turned on the television as Pearson's program was already in progress and watched the big African-American preacher from the hills of West Virginia. As T. D. began to speak about Christ showing His wounds to the apostles, something touched Crouch deep in his soul and he began to weep. Quickly, he picked up the telephone to call Pearson and ask him about this preacher who had such an anointing. Crouch asked him to get Jakes on a plane to Southern California as quickly as possible.

As it turned out, Jakes had been speaking to a friend of his a few days earlier and had expressed his desire to one day have a television ministry. The friend almost mocked him. He reminded T. D. that he wasn't a "big-time preacher," that he did not own any television equipment, and that he did not have a large staff, wealthy church, or anything else that would provide the foundation for a television ministry. Not only that, but who would want to watch? After all, according to his friend, Jakes shouted too much, sweat poured down his face when he preached, and he had that goofy gap in his teeth. His style was all wrong for television. But Jakes's friend also made it clear that, no matter what, T. D. should never let anyone try to change his style.

> Jakes spoke dramatically of Christ showing His wounds to the apostles "Behind Closed Doors" in the house where they had gathered.

Just a few days later, Carlton Pearson called Jakes and told him of the conversation with Paul Crouch. He said that arrangements had been made for T. D. to go to Southern California to meet Crouch and be a guest on the national telecast of *Praise the Lord,* one of the most widely viewed programs on Christian television. As the program was being taped, Paul Crouch told the story of how he happened to view Pearson's program at just the right time to hear this West Virginia preacher reach out and touch his heart.

A few months after he met with Paul Crouch, T. D. was invited to speak at the larger Azusa Conference. Not only was he invited to speak, but he was also asked to preach the final service—the keynote of the entire meeting. In just a few months, T. D. Jakes had gone from being an unknown, cash poor, local preacher to a man rapidly developing a national following and drawing the attention of some of the biggest names in the Christian world. His message at the Azusa Conference would mark the first time T. D. would preach on a national, and even international, stage. This was no seven-minute segment on a television program but an entire sermon delivered live before a worldwide television audience.

T. D. preached the message that had attracted the attention of thousands already: the Sunday school lessons that became the book *Woman, Thou Art Loosed!* He stood nervously backstage; his mouth was dry and the adrenaline was flowing. He fully understood that this was a moment of destiny for him—a moment that would define his life and ministry for many years to come. He later described it this way:

> I was being introduced. But not just to the sizable audience there. I was being introduced to the next twenty years of my living. I was being introduced to the part of me that was waiting in the wings. Ready or not, here I come walking across the stage, taking on the challenge, and being thrust into the brightest blinding light my soul had ever known.[45]

It had been about eleven years since Jakes had started that storefront church. After all those years of digging ditches, working at Union Carbide, living paycheck to paycheck, and struggling to build a church, this was a true moment of harvest.

As Jakes took the pulpit before the large crowd and the international television audience, he began to speak in his signature baritone voice, and the crowd responded. At various moments, people were standing and shouting as if at a sporting event, some with tears streaming down their faces. Thousands of women were jumping, screaming, and crying, because T. D. was speaking and ministering to their pain. And all of it was broadcast live across the nation and in countries around the world.

Soon, T. D. Jakes was speaking to people on his own nationally broadcast television program on TBN, *Get Ready with T. D. Jakes*. It drew an audience of Christians from all ethnicities, denominations, and backgrounds. Jakes was invited to make his telecast available on BET (Black Entertainment Television) as well. His influence was now not just national but also global in reach, as his broadcast was seen in Zimbabwe, South Africa, and England.

For the first two years of his television ministry, Jakes had neither television equipment nor a large staff, but God provided nevertheless. Whenever he would speak at larger churches, he would ask for a copy of the videotape when they recorded the service. He would then have the footage edited and air it on his program. At this time, his only staff members were a secretary and a group of women from his church who volunteered to answer the phones. As much as he acted as though he had a big-time ministry, in reality, T. D. was still believing in the Lord for each step of the way.

Jakes continued to speak at other national charismatic and Pentecostal conferences. In fact, T. D. was receiving more invitations than he could possibly accept. Well-known and respected men, such as R. W. Schambach, Benny Hinn, and Lester Sumrall, were sharing the stage with him. National publications were beginning to take notice as well. *Charisma* magazine published a two-page article about the self-proclaimed "hillbilly from West Virginia."

Woman, Thou Art Loosed! continued to go through printing after printing, staying on the *Publisher's Weekly* Christian best-sellers list for several years. By 2007, it surpassed two million copies sold.

To many people, it appeared as though T. D. Jakes was a phenomenon that happened overnight. Jakes knew, however, that his was a long journey from a brief childhood, through family struggles, to a storefront church with ten people, to a blossoming ministry. It was a journey of growing and maturing as a son, husband, father, pastor, and man. It was a journey of faithfulness in the midst of testing and struggle. It was a journey of one man being true to the call that God had placed on his life, in spite of life's circumstances. It was a journey of listening and responding to the spiritual needs of the people in his church.

> To keep these organizations (the nonprofit T. D. Jakes Ministries and the for-profit T. D. Jakes Enterprises) separate from the church, each operated with its own staff and financial records.

In 1993, Jakes wrote another book, *Can You Stand to Be Blessed?* By 1994, he was conducting over two dozen Woman, Thou Art Loosed conferences each year. T. D. soon addressed the spiritual needs of men by starting a Sunday school class called "Manpower." Just as had happened with the women, these lessons were widely accepted among the men in the community, which led to conferences for men, also called Manpower. The first Manpower conference was held in Detroit for twenty-five hundred men. Soon the conferences were being held at arenas in major cities across America. To minister to the needs of these people, T. D. created both audio and video recordings and provided them for sale at these conferences. He was also writing books on a regular basis. In 1996, T. D. wrote *Loose That Man and Let Him Go!*

Jakes formed separate entities to handle the various functions of his ministry and business. Besides the church, Jakes formed a nonprofit corporation called T. D. Jakes Ministries to produce his conferences, which attended to their preparation, organization, advertising, and publicity. He also formed T. D. Jakes Enterprises, a for-profit entity that produced his books, and eventually his plays and movies as well. To keep these organizations separate from the church, each operated with its own staff and financial records. This arrangement allowed Jakes, and not his church, to assume all of the risk and responsibility for creating events, books, and other endeavors, but it also allowed him to declare and receive any profits created by T. D. Jakes Enterprises.

When T. D. and Serita had self-published *Woman, Thou Art Loosed!*, they had risked the $15,000 they had been saving for a down payment on a house. After just two weeks, the first printing had sold out, and it became a national best seller. At one point, it was selling at the rate of five thousand copies per week. This high rate of sales was unprecedented for a self-published book by an African-American pastor, and provided a level of prosperity that the Jakes family had never imagined and could scarcely believe. T. D. and Serita decided to use some of the money from the book to purchase a very upscale home in Charleston, a city not accustomed to preachers living in fancy houses—especially African-American preachers. It was known locally as the Martin mansion, but the Jakes were also able to purchase the adjoining property to use as a guest house. The home cost over a million dollars and included a bowling alley as well as an outdoor swimming pool and tennis courts. T. D. now wore specially tailored suits and drove a new Mercedes. Serita was wearing upscale fashions with stunning jewelry.

The local Charleston press had a field day discussing their new lifestyle. In a town of only 65,000 people, there is not much that escapes local notice. The gossip and press coverage was fierce. The *Charleston Gazette* criticized him regarding profits from the seminars, implying that Jakes's motive was purely profit-driven rather than spiritual. Estimating a cost of twenty dollars per person at each conference, the publication calculated that he made as much as $360,000 for three days' work—more than one could earn in a lifetime at a chemical plant job. Of course, Jakes didn't pocket the full twenty-dollar conference fee, as there were numerous expenses and rental costs. Any businessman knows there is a big difference between gross and net income in business. This, however, was not reflected in the newspaper's story.

T. D. and Serita felt they had done nothing wrong and had nothing to hide, so they didn't try, but this view was not held by everyone. The *Gazette* didn't let up. Its editor, self-avowed agnostic James Haught, ran a front-page story describing the seven-bedroom home T. D. and Serita had purchased and characterized Jakes as a "young guy caught up in the preaching business" and as someone who was "cashing in."[46] Charleston was not accustomed to their local preachers becoming household names, best-selling authors, and national television personalities. In 1995, a *Gazette* editorial accused T. D. of not obeying the biblical example of living humbly: "Christians and especially ministers should set an example and not live like kings....The love of money is the root of all evil."[47]

> Any businessman knows there is a big difference between gross and net income in business. This, however, was not reflected in the newspaper's story.

T. D. was devastated by the article. It was published as he was hosting a conference that had brought ten thousand people to Charleston, making a major economic impact on the city of around $3 million— which went directly into the pockets of local businessmen and women.

Jakes felt betrayed. He had lived in the Charleston area almost his entire life. He was not someone who had come into the area and taken money from the citizens by deceit and fraud. His story of difficult survival for so many years was not a secret. His parents were also known in the community since his mother had been a teacher and his father a local businessman. But now he was being attacked by the local media, and no one was standing up and defending him. He called a press conference and vented his anger regarding the press, but to little avail.

Jakes later described it this way:

I was successful, which was viewed as wrong in a poor state. And I was black? And I was a preacher? Oh, it was like, "Lunch, boys! Come and eat! Dinner is served!" They were having me for dinner, and I didn't even know I was on the menu.[48]

The newspaper asked him what his congregation would think if they knew he lived this way. He reminded them that there had been a big open house when he'd moved into the home, and that the church members had gone swimming in the pool and had bowled in the alley.

In a state that is only 3 to 4 percent black, it is more polite for critics to deal with the occupational aspect, but there is a degree of racial undertones. Two successful white businessmen lived in the houses before me, and it never made the papers.[49]

Later, the newspaper sent a reporter to his door to ridicule him again for his prosperity. He told the woman of his years of living in substandard housing in poor neighborhoods. He told her that he believed he was an example to others that God would bless His people if they were faithful. He reminded the reporter that the money to purchase the home, the furnishings, the car he drove, and the clothes he wore had not come from contributions made in the offering plates at the church but from his work outside of his pastorate. He claimed that he was like any other businessman who earned money from books, tapes, speaking engagements, and other business ventures. Just as other best-selling authors lived in a style in keeping with their earnings, he did the same. This explanation seemed to have little impact with the reporter. Finally, he said to her, "It was only a few years ago that the media would be interviewing you as a woman because you shouldn't be a reporter. They would say that you should be home making biscuits."[50] She had to admit his words were true.

Even though this was not the end of the articles, Jakes felt that this reporter had begun to understand that much of the issue was that T. D. Jakes had stepped out of the comfort zone of some in the community. He was doing something that others were not accustomed to seeing preachers do. Many assumed that the only way a preacher could achieve such financial gain in his life was by being a crook. Their minds could not conceive of any other way.

Charleston was creating other problems for Jakes and his ministry. He was now bringing conferences to the city that overflowed all of the hotels in the area. There were the Woman, Thou Art Loosed! and Manpower conferences, and later the When Shepherds Bleed conferences for ministers and their spouses. People who could not find hotel rooms were sleeping in their cars. There was no public transportation. Not only was Charleston not appreciative of the business, but the lack of facilities and services was hindering Jakes's ministry. Charleston was simply a small town with small-town amenities. It was not a simple thing to fly to the Charleston airport from other cities. A joke at the time suggested that in order to get to heaven from Charleston you had to go through Pittsburgh. In addition, because of the lack of direct flights to many places, it was difficult and time-consuming for Jakes to maintain a schedule that was becoming increasingly travel dependent. Living in Charleston was not an asset to his ministry.

If Jakes was to continue to conduct his ministry in Charleston, West Virginia, there would have to be some changes. Charleston, however, did not seem open to change. Thus, T. D. began to seek the Lord and ask if there was an open door anywhere that would resolve the problem. He did not want to leave the state of his birth, and the only home he had ever known, but he knew that something had to change for his ministry to grow and become what God intended for it to be.

ENTERING THE POTTER'S HOUSE

I didn't go to Dallas to pastor a megachurch.
My first accountability was to the God
who called me to preach in the first place.

—T. D. Jakes[51]

Chapter Five

ENTERING THE POTTER'S HOUSE

W V. Grant was in big trouble. Born to itinerant evangelist parents, Grant claims to have attended eighty-four different schools in forty-nine states by the time he completed high school. When his father, Dr. W. V. Grant Sr., died in 1983, Grant took over the church he had started in the Oak Cliff area of Dallas, Soul's Harbor Church. He renamed the church Eagle's Nest Cathedral and in 1987 purchased twenty-eight acres of land in the southwest section of Dallas. There he built Eagle's Nest Family Church, a huge facility with a five-thousand-seat auditorium where he held services and televised faith healing meetings. That's when things began to go wrong.

In 1991, Grant was featured in an investigative report by Diane Sawyer for ABC-TV's *Prime Time Live*. The program exposed members of Grant's staff circulating among the audience before the service and selecting people in advance who had specific problems and ailments. They would speak to Grant through tiny microphones while he was on stage, and he would then "miraculously" call out information about these people that he claimed came from the Holy Spirit. That exposé was followed by a similar segment for the CBS program *60 Minutes*.

A few years later, Grant was taped by the IRS taking money raised to feed starving children and using it to purchase a $1.9 million mansion. Grant and his third wife, Brenda, had transferred $100,000 of ministry funds to a personal account, which they used as a down payment. Because they had not reported the money as taxable income, Grant was indicted for tax fraud. The indictment, combined with the healing exposés, had destroyed what was left of his ministry. In 1996, Grant was convicted of tax fraud and sentenced to sixteen months in federal prison.

In the spring of 1996, T. D. Jakes received a phone call from Grant, who had his large Dallas church up for sale. It was quite an opportunity. The church building not only had a huge auditorium, but it also had classrooms, offices, and enough parking for a large church. It was conveniently located near a major freeway.

At first, Jakes encouraged another pastor friend in Dallas to purchase the property, but then he woke up one night with a start. He knew something had to change if his ministry was going to prosper.

> I really felt that it was a sovereign move of God. It wasn't an intellectual choice. On my own accord, I would not have chosen that particular city; not that I had any likes or dislikes—I just didn't know a lot about Dallas.[52]

Jakes had been preaching services in the Dallas area about once a month, and his ministry had always been warmly received there. Dallas was the location of one of the largest TBN studios in the country. It was the host site of as much locally produced programming as any of their stations in the country, with the exception of the mother station in southern California. Also, Dallas was a city with a great deal of wealth. It was home to several corporations and individuals who had made great fortunes in the oil industry. There were also numerous large corporations who did business in technology, manufacturing, and finance.

Dallas was the ninth largest city in the United States and the fifth largest metropolitan area. It was also a very diverse city ethnically and racially, with about 50 percent of the population white, and the other 50 percent divided among African-Americans, Native Americans, Asians, and a fast-growing Hispanic population. This was a city where a large ministry and an affluent pastor would not stand out like a sore thumb amidst the mix of large churches and prosperous citizens.

At that time, Jakes's church in Charleston had an attendance of about a thousand, and it continued to attract a very diverse crowd, with about 35 percent of the congregation white. The demographic makeup of Charleston, however, severely limited the ability of the church to grow. Charleston had about fifty thousand people. Therefore, Jakes's church represented about 2 percent of the population of the city. Among all of the megachurches in America today, there is not a single one that is able to reach even 1 percent of its city's population, including Lakewood Church in Houston, Texas, Saddleback Community Church in Orange County, California, or Willow Creek Community Church in South Barrington, Illinois.

> After all was said and done, fifty Charleston families decided to relocate with Jakes to Dallas and help him plant a new church.

T. D. Jakes and his ministry were already making a major impact in Charleston, but further growth from this point forward would be difficult. It certainly seemed that Jakes had outgrown Charleston in every way. T. D. admitted as much when he said, "I have always been somebody outside of the box, especially when the box is small. And that was a small box."[53]

Jakes agreed to purchase Grant's property for $3.2 million, and then sat down with his church in Charleston to share his vision for what God had in store for them. After all was said and done, fifty families decided to relocate with Jakes to Dallas and help him plant a new church. These families would become the backbone of the church, filling staff positions, mostly on a volunteer basis in the beginning, with hopes that ,if things went well, the jobs would turn into paid positions.

Entering the Potter's House

There were really three reasons for the move. First, Jakes felt that he had done everything he could do in Charleston, and recently he had hit the ceiling of potential there. Second, he already had a working relationship with the TBN studio operation there. Third, the Dallas-Fort Worth International Airport was one of the biggest airline hubs in the country, which allowed large groups of people to come and go for conferences much more easily. The Dallas/Fort Worth population was twice as large as the entire state of West Virginia, and the infrastructure was much more conducive to large meetings than West Virginia would ever be.[54]

Jakes prepared himself for the tough job of, once again, starting over and building a church from the ground up. "I came here fully expecting to go through the long road of building from the grass roots. I have done that before."[55] He renamed the church The Potter's House, taken from Jeremiah 18:4: *"And the vessel that he made of clay was marred in the hand of the potter; so he made it again into another vessel, as it seemed good to the potter to make."*

Jakes purchased the large facility in order to handle the thousands of people who attended his conferences. The thought was that even if they didn't fill the church on Sundays, they would fill it for the conferences. On their very first Sunday in Dallas, however, fifteen hundred people came to The Potter's House. The number of people who joined The Potter's House on that first Sunday was larger than their entire congregation had been in Charleston. Those who had moved with Jakes were amazed. In Charleston, if a dozen people joined the church on one Sunday it was a good day. On their first Sunday in Dallas, they had seen more than a hundred times that number make a commitment to be a part of the new church.

Jakes was as surprised as anyone with the response they received in Dallas. Later he would describe his perspective to the National Association of Black Journalists. "I didn't go to Dallas to pastor a megachurch.

My first accountability was to God, who called me to preach in the first place." He went on to say that the overwhelming success was "something I couldn't have predicted."[56]

Immediately, The Potter's House was one of the fastest-growing churches in America. The word quickly spread: T. D. Jakes had moved to Dallas to start a brand new church, and it was exploding. T. D.'s television program was going out across the cable and broadcast networks around the country where they announced the new location on a weekly basis.

Despite what Jakes may have thought when he went to Dallas, he was not able to duck the media attention when he purchased a large home in an affluent Dallas neighborhood. The home, located in the White Lake section of Dallas, had seven bedrooms, was nearly ten thousand square feet, and was located next door to the former home of the late H. L. Hunt, an oil tycoon who was once regarded as the richest man in the country. Jakes paid $1.7 million for the home, about half the price of the entire church facility. He quickly found out that even in a major media market, it was not that easy to be inconspicuous.

To say that T. D. Jakes and The Potter's House made a big splash in Dallas is an understatement. They immediately began to establish unique ministries not found in most churches. They quickly announced that The Potter's House would be establishing a local restoration center that would house programs for overcoming many types of abuse, among them sexual, chemical, and emotional.

In March 1998, ground was broken for the City of Refuge, a 231-acre complex near the church, which would offer rehabilitation, education, and training for those in need. Among those present at the ground-breaking ceremony was Texas governor and future president George W. Bush, as well as Dallas mayor Ron Kirk. The goal of the City of Refuge was "to build an environment where spirituality could develop and flourish in the lives of needy people after basic life essentials, such as food and shelter, had been met."[57] Jakes proclaimed, "If you're pushing drugs on the street and you're any good at it, that means you are a skilled salesman. What we want to do is take that skill and turn it around."[58]

An important part of the City of Refuge was what was called the "business incubator," an educational facility providing classes on business and management. Those completing the business course would present a business plan. Those whose plans were considered viable were assisted in obtaining funds to make the plans become a reality. For others, job and financial assistance came in the form of professional clothing, help with interview skills, or learning how to obtain a bank loan.

The racially diverse approach to ministry at The Potter's House was also something Dallas had not seen before on this scale. Many churches had people of more than one race or ethnic background, but to have nearly a third of the congregation made up of races different from that of the senior pastor was not common at all, especially for an African-American pastor. It was generally assumed that white Christians would not follow an African-American pastor's leadership in large numbers. The Potter's House proved this idea wrong from the very beginning.

> Jakes proclaimed, "If you're pushing drugs on the street and you're any good at it, that means you are a skilled salesman. What we want to do is take that skill and turn it around."

The growth of the church was stunning to both those who moved with Jakes to Dallas and the church world in general. The group from West Virginia was accustomed to living and ministering in a small town with a rural culture where things moved slowly and there would always be time to finish what didn't get done today. They had to quickly acclimate to an urban environment. T. D. spoke of some of the things they had to learn almost overnight.

The quick growth was a big shock, but the urban issues as well. I had been pastoring 20 years, so I was well-experienced in the day-to-day challenges, but they are compounded by the inner-city demographics. They were complex, but they were motivating. I jumped in with both feet.[59]

JAKES AND COWBOYS

One of the things that impacted the new church in a major way came from an unexpected area. Dallas had always been one of the biggest sports cities in the country. Besides having teams in professional baseball, hockey, basketball, and soccer, it also had what has been dubbed "America's team," the NFL's Dallas Cowboys. The Cowboys have always been much like a religion in Dallas. Everything they do is news, in season and out. Everywhere members of the team go, and every word they speak, is immediately spread across the papers and airwaves of the city and surrounding area.

T. D. was now doing less of the "hands on" counseling in the church due to his writing and speaking. Among those he brought with him from West Virginia were people who counseled couples about their relationships. However, when Carolyn Chambers Sanders phoned the church office, the call was put directly through to Jakes himself.

Carolyn was the wife of the all-pro cornerback of the Dallas Cowboys, Deion Sanders. "Neon Deion," as he was called, was one of the best known, most flamboyant, and highly outspoken football players in the country, who never turned down an opportunity for a media interview. He had led two different teams in the NFL to the Super Bowl. He was also one of the most feared punt and kick returners in the league.

Carolyn had heard about the influence that Jakes seemed to have on both men and women across the country. She believed that her husband was in desperate need of Jakes's influence. Deion's skills as a husband did not measure up to the skills he exhibited on the playing field. His lifestyle was spiraling out of control. He was yielding to the temptations that are always available to a man of his fame and abilities. It seemed that anyone and everyone was willing to feed Deion's ego and tell him whatever he wanted to hear. What he needed was someone to help him become grounded in what was real in life, like his faith and family. He needed someone who would not be blinded by the money, fame, and spotlights, someone who would shoot straight and speak the truth to him. That kind of help was not available from his biological father or stepfather, for they had both passed away. Carolyn knew that if her marriage had any hope of survival, her husband needed this kind of strong male influence in his life. From all she had seen and heard, Bishop T. D. Jakes was just the man to provide that influence.

> Jakes began to encourage Deion to put away his self-indulgent ways and not to believe everything that his entourage was telling him.

When Carolyn and Deion Sanders went to Jakes for marriage counseling, Deion was immediately taken with Jakes. Here was a man who was in Deion's tax bracket and not ashamed of it. In his own way, Jakes was just as flamboyant as Deion was. He lived in a wealthy neighborhood and drove an expensive car. He was unlike any pastor Deion had ever known, but he still upheld strong standards regarding the importance of faith and family. Jakes began to encourage Deion to put away his self-indulgent ways and not to believe everything that his entourage was telling him.

Deion bought into Jakes, The Potter's House, the Bible, and the need to change his life. After several meetings with T. D., Deion accepted Jesus Christ as his Savior and quickly became an enthusiastic participant in the Sunday services, the Wednesday night Bible study, and his one-on-one sessions with Jakes. Deion's way of life totally changed. He seemed to accept the ways of God with the same enthusiasm that he embraced athletics and fame. Deion later said, "The ministry was like a life raft, and it saved me."[60]

Deion didn't come alone. Soon, the Cowboys' all-pro running back and NFL all-time rushing leader, Emmitt Smith, began to attend as well. He was taken by the messages he heard from the pulpit. Smith said, "When I went to The Potter's House and heard Bishop preach every week, every Bible study, the message was so strong and so power-ful you could not sit in that house and not be changed."[61] Jakes soon assumed a strong fatherly role with Emmitt, as well, who was not shy about letting people know about his association with Jakes.

> He's a normal person. He laughs. He jokes. He likes to check out movies. We try to have lunch once in a while....I love the man because spiritually he's right on and he's definitely in touch spiritually, and he's even more impressive when you get to know him personally. To me, it's just like a father talking to a son, and I appreciate it.[62]

Deion Sanders, Emmitt Smith, and all-pro wide receiver Michael Irvin were all baptized at The Potter's House in October 1997. Also baptized were teammates Omar Stoutmire and George Hegiman. As Emmitt came up out of the water, he raised his hands as if he was scor-ing a touchdown. Deion did a little two-step in the water as he was baptized. George Hegiman, a 314-pound offensive lineman, definitely displaced the most water from the baptistery. After the service, the players huddled together, weeping.

The Potter's House did not inform the media of the baptisms prior to the ceremony, as everyone involved wanted to preserve the sanctity of the moment. A video of the baptism, however, was created by the minis-try and was made available to all of Dallas' broadcast media, as well as to many of the sports highlight shows across the country. All of this took place less than eighteen months after T. D. Jakes had moved to Dallas and started The Potter's House.

In the coming months, Jakes continued to nurture his relationship with these athletes, taking them with him to Promise Keepers or other conferences as their schedules would permit. Certainly, it did not hurt T. D.'s nationally growing reputation to have some high-profile celebrities in the congregation. During a revival crusade in Birmingham, Jakes explained to the audience that when he began counseling Sanders, he told the Cowboys star that becoming a Christian did not mean he had to change his flamboyant personality. "To deny him that would be to deny him who he is as a person. If I'm going to be flashy and flamboyant, I'd like to do it for the Lord."[63]

Jakes often uses Sanders and Smith as illustrations in his sermons. "Deion Sanders and Emmitt Smith had money and were not happy. The biblical teaching about prosperity is much more than dollars and cents."[64] In doing so, Jakes addresses an inner conflict that many men of faith face: the need to be successful yet also men of God. T. D. brought financially successful men before his congregation and declared that being financially successful and loving God were not mutually exclusive. "Real men" could do both. For Jakes, the issue is not whether a person can be financially successful; the issue is whether that person can be faithful with what the Lord gives him or her. *Moreover it is required in stewards that one be found faithful* (1 Corinthians 4:2). In April 1998, when the time came for The Potter's House to build its new auditorium, Deion Sanders was faithful, reportedly contributing one million dollars to the cause.[65]

> For Jakes, the issue is not whether a person can be financially successful; the issue is whether that person can be faithful with what the Lord gives him or her.

Although Sanders' relationship with Jakes and The Potter's House continued, his marriage did not. Deion and Carolyn Sanders were divorced in 1997. Jakes later officiated at Deion's second marriage to New York actress and model Pilar Biggers in the Bahamas in 1999. Jakes continues to serve as a counselor to both Deion and Emmitt.

MANAGING GROWTH

A million dollars for a new auditorium was just a small part of what it took to build The Potter's House. By 1998, the church had exploded and was turning away as many as five hundred people each week from three overflowing weekend services. The first thought was to simply expand the original auditorium by "blowing out" the side walls. This seemed to be the quickest and most cost-effective solution. Engineers, however, ran computer-generated studies that showed that having large numbers of seats would compromise sightlines due to the existence of load-bearing walls. When faced with this reality, the decision was made to build an entirely new auditorium.

A design team was directed to draw up plans for a facility that could seat at least eight thousand people, with an altar area that could accommodate at least five hundred. This directive created a number of problems, beginning with the distance needed between the pulpit and the people. To solve the problem, the plans called for the stage to be raised and twenty by twenty-six foot, 12,000-lumen video screens to be included to provide intimate and clear pictures of the stage to the entire room.

The Potter's House moved into its new facility in October 2000. In just four years in Dallas, it had grown from fifty families to a claim of over twenty-five thousand members. But T. D. Jakes's vision was the same.

Our vision for The Potter's House is to meet the culture at the point of its need, and the twenty-first century brings new challenges and opportunities. The church must deliver a relevant message and life-impacting programs. It must become more user-friendly, and the church leadership must keep open minds about creative ways to embrace the larger communit love.[66]

The thirty-two-million-dollar facility was built most cutting-edge technical innovations of any church building in the United States. The first four rows of the sanctuary were completely interactive, giving people the ability to immediately download sermons and Power Point presentations. Handheld computer devices used by altar attendants allowed for the immediate input of new member data and prayer requests. The 191,000-square-foot facility held 8,425 people, with an overflow chapel providing an additional capacity of five hundred when needed. The choir loft held up to three hundred choir members as well as a forty-five-piece orchestra. There was a language translation center with the capacity for six simultaneous translations received through wireless headphones, which were available in the lobby.

> The thirty-two-million-dollar facility was built with some of the most cutting-edge technical innovations of any church building in the United States.

Another consideration in the new facility was the television ministry. With the number of programs broadcast weekly around the world, the auditorium would be a constant source of video of the ministry. Although weekly sermons would be taped and edited for the various programs, Jakes did not want the auditorium to have the feel of a television studio. The designers and architects worked diligently to overcome this problem. One of the solutions to creating an inviting atmosphere while still accommodating the technical needs was to paint the ceiling with clouds to hide the catwalks, audio, video, and lighting equipment.

When the new auditorium was dedicated, it created a sensation around the country in both the religious and political worlds. Among those present was Coretta Scott King, who reminded the congregation, "A church is not measured by the beauty of the architecture, but by the deeds of the congregation." Vice President Al Gore, who was running for president at the time, as well as television evangelist Pat Robertson, also addressed the celebration. Gore, who came despite criticism from some liberal pundits for addressing a conservative Christian audience, spoke to the crowd for eighteen minutes, reciting portions of a hymn, paraphrasing two Bible stories, and quoting the Scriptures four times. The *New York Times* reported on the event, saying, "In both content and tone, [Gore] waded into waters usually reserved for Republican politicians, a point made explicit by the presence at the same service of Pat Robertson, the Christian Coalition founder."[67] Republican candidate George W. Bush, unable to attend due to a previous commitment, sent a proclamation of support, as did President Bill Clinton and Dallas mayor Ron Kirk.

When the new auditorium was completed, The Potter's House had a total debt of forty-five million dollars. In just over three years, however, the entire debt was paid off in full. The church paid over a million dollars a month, on average, toward the principal of the mortgage and was able to completely wipe out the debt.

EDUCATION

One of the closest things to the heart of T. D. Jakes is education. Because of the heritage established by his mother, he understands the importance of education and how it can better a person's life. Much of the emphasis of The Potter's House is on education for both adults and young people. There is education for adults to provide them with the resources to get a GED if they dropped out of high school. There is the Potter's House School of Ministry, a six-month course for those considering full-time ministry. There is The Potter's Institute, which helps people mold their character through knowledge, understanding, and application of godly principles in businesses, communities, and the lives of families.

Perhaps the most impressive, however, is Clay Academy for children and young people, a Christian school for grades K–9, which has plans to add a high school in the near future. T. D. has said that he wants Clay Academy to be an example of high graduation-to-college rates, technology infusion, performing arts, and world-class athletics. There are strict guidelines regarding appearance; students are required to wear uniforms.

In the fall of 2006, Clay Academy dedicated its first permanent building, a 70,000-square-foot facility. Dallas mayor Laura Miller was the keynote speaker at the dedication and was clearly impressed with the campus. "With Bishop Jakes's national and international reputation, I think it will build volumes and bring

> "A church is not measured by the beauty of the architecture, but by the deeds of the congregation."
> —Coretta Scott King

a lot of people here to Dallas, just to see this place." Currently, there are plans to build six additional buildings, including a performing arts center, chapel, amphitheater, middle school, elementary school, gymnasium, and cafeteria. Before the first building was completed, the school met in everything from trailers in the church parking lot to a former supermarket. Now the two hundred thirty students have a campus that would be the envy of many small colleges. Tuition ranges from $5,200 to $6,700, depending upon the grade level of the student.

WOMAN TO WOMAN

Serita Jakes has developed the Woman to Woman ministry, which reaches out to women at every stage of life. As for her motivation, Serita said,

I wanted to establish relationships. I find that women often have a problem identifying and relating to women. We're often intimidated by one another. We're often very critical of one another. I wanted to rip the veil and just deal with women relationally—mother to daughter, sister to sister.[68]

One part of the ministry is the Debutante Program for teenaged girls with a B average or better in school. The mentoring program was inspired by Isaiah 47:7, which says, *"And you said, 'I shall be a lady forever,' so that you did not take these things to heart, nor remember the latter end of them."* Each girl commits every other Saturday of the month to the program.

It is Serita's attempt to defy the contemporary culture where girls tend to dress in baggy jeans or revealing attire. In the Debutante Program, a young woman is treated to a manicure, a pedicure, and a new outfit, usually a suit with lace or pearls on it. Serita also teaches the young women table etiquette; they are treated to a meal at a fine restaurant to practice their skills. In addition, the young women are encouraged to make a commitment to abstain from sex until they are married. If they have been the victims of rape or abuse, a professional counselor is brought in to assist in the healing process. At the end of the twelve-week program, there is a service at The Potter's House where each young woman receives an autographed copy of T. D. Jakes's book, *Daddy Loves His Girls*, as well as a Bible with Serita's name inscribed inside.

The Debutante Program is not free. Each applicant must pay a nonrefundable application processing fee of $150. In addition, there is a renewal fee to participate each year. Each girl is required to provide her most recent report card, two letters of reference from teachers or school counselors, a one-page, typed letter from a parent or guardian stating why her application should be considered, and a one-page, typed document from the applicant stating her interests, hobbies, and aspirations. She is also to give a testimony regarding her salvation experience.

Entering the Potter's House

MINISTRY FOR MEN

Well over 40 percent of The Potter's House membership is male. Among the ministries for them is one of the largest men's chorales in the country. Men may also serve as part of a large squad of ushers, who direct everything around the church before, during, and after each service. It is not difficult to find these men, as they are neatly attired in sharp suits with beautiful dress shirts, matching ties, and handkerchiefs. Jakes has strived to create a church where it is comfortable to be known as a man of God. These men understand their role in the lives of their wives, children, and extended families.

> Jakes has strived to create a church where it is comfortable to be known as a man of God.

There is also a group called AMEN, an acronym for Adullam Men's Empowerment Network. The name comes from a passage in 1 Samuel:

> *David therefore departed from there and escaped to the cave of Adullam. And when his brothers and all his father's house heard it, they went down there to him. And everyone who was in distress, everyone who was in debt, and everyone who was discontented gathered to him. So he became captain over them. And there were about four hundred men with him.* (1 Samuel 22:1–2)

Adullam was a safe haven for David and his men when they were running from King Saul. Similarly, AMEN is a men's mentor program and place of safe haven for men in need of vision and restoration The ministry was founded in January 1999 and, through today, has involved ten thousand five hundred men, including a four-hundred-voice choir.

COUNSELING CENTER

The Potter's House has a counseling center that provides people with a safe place for professional counseling, spiritual guidance, and education that bring healing, reconciliation, and hope during times of personal or family crisis. Mental health professionals, marriage and family therapists, chemical dependency counselors, and lay volunteers staff the center, which also consults with outside psychologists, psychiatrists, and family doctors. Among the services the center provides are marriage and newlywed seminars, Christ-centered 12-step programs, and a ministry called Fresh Oil, an intense counseling ministry for out-of-town visitors who need healing, restoration, and a fresh encounter with God.

BIBLE TRAINING

There are several ministries at The Potter's House devoted to helping people become grounded in the Word of God. One of those ministries is called Brick House, an in-depth Bible study on divine purpose, sex, finances, and stewardship in the community. This ministry helps facilitate individual growth (the bricks) and prepares people for their journey to build the kingdom of God (the house).

There are also strong children's and youth ministries. Destiny House ministers to children through discipleship classes, small group participation, children's church, mentor programs, community outreach, and special events. Fire House is committed to reclaiming, retrieving, and restoring the lives of young people and helping them to become visionaries who can empower others. A portion of Fire House is called Project Take Over (PTO), whose goal is to create and stimulate young people's awareness of their identity in Jesus Christ. PTO is committed to bringing back morals and values in schools, communities, homes, and businesses.

Another part of the biblical education ministry is The Potter's Institute, established in September 2000. This school is not an accredited degree-granting institution, but certificates of completion are awarded to students who complete their studies in various topical areas. The mission is to "develop a disciple's character in knowledge and understanding of Godly life principles through applied teaching for the betterment of their community, family, and personal life, that God's kingdom be established on earth." The classes meet at various times through the week in six five-week terms each year. The Institute offers classes in several areas including Doctrine and Theology, Essentials of Christian Living, Great Books of the Bible, Financial Freedom, Kingdom Principles and Preparation, Leadership, and Relationships.

Prison Ministry

The Potter's House also has a powerful prison ministry called New Creation Prison and Jail Ministry. Church members reach out to imprisoned individuals to help them restore their lives through the infusion of intellectual, emotional, and spiritual influences. The goal is to help the incarcerated to discard harmful patterns and attitudes, avoid destructive relationships and behavior, stay out of prison, and become positive contributors to society. In addition to working in the prison environment, the ministry provides support groups at The Potter's House to assist men and women after their release in restructuring their identities in an atmosphere of acceptance. There are also family support groups for individuals who have family members or significant others who are incarcerated. The Potter's House has invested over half a million dollars in this outreach.

Outreach Ministries

During the 2003 Manpower Conference, church members and visitors built two Habitat for Humanity homes and donated $107,000 to relocate some Dallas citizens from an economically and environmentally disadvantaged area. The Potter's House was also responsible for building a hospital in Belize; it later sent $400,000 for medical supplies.

ARTS MINISTRIES

The Potter's House also has thriving arts ministries, including the Before His Throne Dance Ministry. This group not only dances during times of worship, but it also holds conferences to assist other churches in developing dance ministries. These conferences include sessions on such topics as praise and worship dance, hip-hop, modern dance, and ethnic African and Jewish dances.

NATIONALLY RANKED

The Potter's House is one of the largest congregations in the United States. In a 2004 issue of *Outreach* magazine, which listed the one hundred largest churches in America, The Potter's House was listed as the fourth largest church, and the third fastest growing. The list reported a weekly attendance of 18,500, with a growth of 11,300 people during 2003.[69]

In the 2005 issue, The Potter's House was listed as the ninth largest congregation in America. Not bad for a church in its ninth year. On the other hand, they were no longer on the magazine's list of the top 100 fastest-growing churches.[70] In the 2006 issue, they were listed as the twentieth largest church in the country and the twenty-fifth fastest growing.[71] Obviously, by 2006, growth at the church was no longer as explosive as it had been in the first few years as the weekly attendance had leveled off. When the 2007 numbers were released, however, The Potter's House had jumped to the ninth largest church and the thirtieth fastest growing.[72]

Maintaining a congregation of this size is obviously no easy task. In such a church, hundreds of people are constantly moving for other job opportunities, getting married, having children, or passing away. To simply maintain a weekly attendance of this size, a church consistently would need to add hundreds of people to replace those who leave for various reasons. The church staff must be organized to minister to the steady flow of new faces coming in the doors, as well as to continue to care for those who have been there for years.

In January 2006, *The Church Report* announced its list of the "Top Fifty Most Influential Churches" in America. The list was compiled by highly respected church growth expert John Vaughan, who surveyed two thousand church leaders with the goal of ranking the most influential churches among those with more than two thousand in attendance. Of the one hundred and twenty-seven churches that received votes as most influential, The Potter's House ranked eighth on the survey. It was the highest ranked church on the list pastored by an African-American, and the second highest ranked charismatic church—the other being Joel Osteen's Lakewood Church in Houston. At only ten years in existence, The Potter's House was also the youngest church on the list.[73]

Despite its rapid growth and its increasing exposure to the spotlight, Jakes's ministry has remained focused.

> We're commanded by the Scriptures to deny the flesh from having control and to allow Christ to rule. But we often struggle to see who is going to reign. That's the reality we grapple with each day. Having the freedom to acknowledge that—and making the commitment to mature through it—is what [my ministry] is all about.[74]

Democratic presidential candidate Vice President Al Gore, right, laughs with Bishop T. D. Jakes, left, as his wife Serita Jakes sits in the middle during the dedication service for the Potter's House sanctuary, a multiracial non-denominational church, Sunday, 22 October 2000 in Dallas. (AP Photo/Pablo Martinez Monsivais)

Former UN Ambassador Andrew Young, right, and Rev. T. D. Jakes listen during the Coretta Scott King funeral ceremony at the New Birth Missionary Baptist Church in Lithonia, GA, Tuesday, 7 February 2006. (AP Photo/ Ric Feld, Pool)

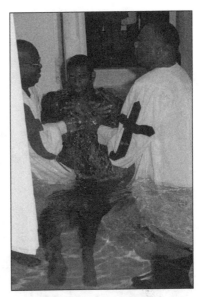

Dallas Cowboys players Emmitt Smith, center in left photo, and Deion Sanders, center in right photo, are baptized by Bishop T. D. Jakes, shown on the right in each image, during a ceremony at The Potter's House Church in Dallas, Sunday, 19 October 1997. (AP Photo/A. Larry Ross and Associates Inc, Booker T. Gracey)

Bishop T. D. Jakes of Dallas, Texas, delivers his sermon to a near-capacity crowd of mostly women, Thursday, 29 July 1999, at the Georgia Dome in Atlanta, as he begins his 1999 Woman, Thou Art Loosed Conference. (AP Photo/Bill Cranford)

THE NATIONAL STAGE

I'm not the next Billy Graham. Why be a cheap copy
of a great original? I'd rather produce new great
originals—people of accomplishment, working
in the trenches of life, touching others.

—T. D. Jakes[75]

Chapter Six

THE NATIONAL STAGE

In a very short period of time, T. D. Jakes had gone from being a big fish in a little pond to a being a big fish in a very big ocean. In less than two years, he went from being a relative unknown to being an easily recognized pastor with a best-selling book and an international television and radio ministry. In a period of less than four years, he went from being the pastor of a local church in a small, fairly rural city, to leading a national ministry in one of the largest metropolitan cities in the country.

For many, it was as though this African-American preacher had fallen to earth from the sky. When he hit the national stage, it was as if everyone became aware if him at once. The American press, both secular and Christian, began to proclaim his accomplishments while trying to discover who he was and where he had come from.

In May 1994, *Charisma* magazine published a two-page article about T. D. Jakes and his ministry and history. The article gave details about this man who was gaining more and more fame to a Christian world hungry for information about him.

Jakes's rise to the national stage put him in a position of influence among leaders in both the religious and political arenas. When Bill Clinton was mired in the Monica Lewinsky scandal, he called some of the most prominent religious leaders in America to the White House, seeking spiritual guidance during this difficult time. Among those religious leaders was T. D. Jakes. This White House meeting, which occurred a short time after Jakes had moved his ministry to Dallas, created a great deal of controversy at the time. Many on the evangelical right had long condemned Bill Clinton and were now calling for his impeachment. They were heavily critical of any pastors who accepted Clinton's invitation. Jakes, however, was never one to shy away from controversy.

In 1999, late in the second term of President Clinton, Jakes served as the keynote speaker for the National Day of Prayer in Washington. Once again, Jakes was on a national stage before the country's religious and civic leaders, not to mention a media that generally seemed interested in charismatic leaders only when they were involved in scandals such as Jim Bakker's or Jimmy Swaggart's. Jakes provided a new model of the charismatic preacher—one who was articulate and scandal free.

In many ways, 2000 was a turning point for Jakes and his ministry. He went from being a rising figure in charismatic and Pentecostal circles as a televangelist and pastor who occasionally surfaced in media articles, to being a man of prominence in the broader national arena. During that year, Jakes served as the keynote speaker at three of the most prestigious conferences for African-Americans: The National Conference of Black Mayors, The National Black Police Association, and the Congressional Black Caucus.

9/11

A few days after the attack on the World Trade Center and the Pentagon on September 11, 2001, President Bush asked Timothy Goeglein, deputy director of White House public liaison, to organize a meeting of religious leaders from around the country. Twenty-seven leaders were invited, including thirteen evangelicals. Among those invited were evangelists Luis Palau and Franklin Graham; pastors Max Lucado, Bill Hybels, and Charles Blake; Cardinal Edward Egan of New York; and T. D. Jakes.

Once inside the White House, the religious leaders were taken to the Roosevelt Room where a circle of chairs had been set up. President Bush's chair was vacant, and no one sat next to it. When Bush came into the room, he jokingly complained of being lonely. The cardinal and Greek Orthodox archbishop Demetrios Trakatellis moved and sat next to him. President Bush spoke to the group informally and recalled talking to Billy Graham at his family's vacation home in Maine when the gospel became real to him for the first time and his life was changed.[76]

Jakes would later publish a sermon regarding the impact of 9/11. In it he explained how he was traveling and was in the Midwest late in the evening on September 10 after ministering in another part of the nation. He awoke the next morning, as much of the nation did, to video of the planes crashing into the twin towers. Not yet fully realizing the significance of all that had happened, he became stranded in Arizona while en route to fulfill another commitment when the FAA closed the nation's airports. In his sermon, Jakes described the grief of a country that had slept while the enemy had strategized, structured, and planned its attack. He called on Christians to unite in prayer behind the president. He called on the Christians of America to awaken, get on their knees, and assault the demonic forces behind the attack with spiritual warfare on a level never seen before. He also clarified that the physical enemy was not those who followed the Islamic religion but those who performed evil acts in the name of religion. This was not a time for bigotry against other religions but a time to raise up the name of Jesus Christ in order to promote what is good and just.[77]

> Jakes was one of most prominent religious leaders in America to encourage Christians to take a spiritual approach to a demonic issue.

The National Stage

Jakes was one of most prominent religious leaders in America to encourage Christians to take a spiritual approach to a demonic issue. He clearly saw the issue as not only social and political, but also one of good versus evil, and he called for Americans to stand up on the side of good.

A NEW MODEL FOR CHARISMATIC CHRISTIANITY

Over the years, Jakes has repeatedly been referred to in both print and broadcast media as the most prominent African-American religious leader in America. Quite often, the phrase *African-American* is omitted, and he is just referred to as "the most prominent religious leader in America." He has frequently been mentioned or interviewed by CNN, *Newsweek, U.S. News & World Report,* and *USA Today,* as well as the various broadcast networks. When major issues arise that require comment from prominent religious leaders, Jakes is almost always on the media's list.

The American secular media has tended to portray Christians as either wild-eyed radicals or ignorant and unsophisticated. When the *Washington Post* described viewers of *The 700 Club* as less educated than most Americans, Pat Robertson challenged this statement. When asked for his source of information, the *Post* reporter's reply was "common knowledge." Only when provided with proof to the contrary did *The Post* admit its error and print a retraction. Faced with this attitude, Jakes has presented an image of the conservative Christian as thoughtful and deliberate. He does not come across as non-judgmental but appears to be open minded toward various viewpoints on the problems of our society.

In 2002, Jakes assisted in fund-raising for one of the most respected African-American charities in the country when he joined Yolanda Adams and Debbie Allen as cohost of *Lou Rawls' Miracle of Stars,* benefiting the United Negro College Fund. The show raises support for thirty-nine historically black colleges and universities across the nation, most of which are found in the southern part of the United States. Among the colleges supported is Tuskegee University, the school Odith Jakes graduated from.

That same year Jakes delivered the keynote address for the regional convention in Dallas of the NAACP, one of the most prominent civil rights organizations in the country. In 2002, Jakes not only was listed in *Who's Who among African-Americans*, but he was also asked to write the foreword for the publication.

In 2005, well-known church polling expert George Barna published a report on those whom pastors considered to have the most influence on churches in America. Evangelist Billy Graham led the list of the top ten, which was to be expected. Jakes was sixth, behind Graham, Saddleback Community Church pastor Rick Warren, President George W. Bush, family advocate James Dobson, and Willow Creek Community Church pastor Bill Hybels. When only the opinions of African-Americans were considered, Jakes was third on the list. He was also third when only the opinions of Pentecostals were considered.

Earlier that same year, *Time* had listed the "25 Most Influential Evangelicals in America." The list included pastors, evangelists, broadcasters, and politicians. Jakes was number six on this list as well. *Time* described Jakes in this way:

> A master of pop psychology, Jakes...represents a new wrinkle for Evangelicals, the neo-Pentecostals, who combine intense spirituality with a therapeutic approach.[78]

Jakes continued to be recognized by groups all over the country. In April 2005, he was honored as a Trumpet Award recipient. In June of the same year, he was awarded the Chairman's Award for Community Empowerment by 100 Black Men of America, Inc. He won the 2006 Quill Award in the Religion/Spirituality category for his best-selling book, *Mama Made the Difference*.

In 2005, Jakes was named cochairman of the committee commissioned to oversee the distribution of government and charity funds after the Hurricane Katrina disaster. Soon afterward, in his keynote message at the National Day of Prayer, Jakes spoke of how Katrina "made us think and look and reach beyond the breach and dare to discuss the unmentionable issues that confront us."[79] Later in the message, he seemed to be speaking directly to President Bush.

> It is not so important what we say; it is important what we do. Defining moments of history cannot be defined by rhetoric and words or anger, or soliciting people to respond in a tempestuous way. But real leadership is defined by what we do. The Good Samaritan teaches us that it will cost money to help people, and sometimes we have to love them enough to pay the bill.[80]

CIVIL RIGHTS, POLITICS, AND RACE

During the latter part of the 1990s, Jakes began to be mentioned more in public discussions about civil rights. Some publications, both religious and secular, began to call him a civil rights leader. He obviously had not been a part of the civil rights leadership that has been prominent in this country since the 1950s in the traditions of Martin Luther King Jr., Jesse Jackson, and Andrew Young. Yet Jakes has been influenced somewhat by the legacy of Dr. King. Jakes has a connection with King through his mother, who went to high school with Coretta Scott King. She and Mrs. King remained friends throughout their lives. In many ways, Jakes represents a new generation of leaders in the African-American community.

Jakes is different because he has not aligned himself with the Democratic Party as many black leaders have. He has always kept himself apolitical, making friends with both Republicans and Democrats. In doing so, Jakes has been criticized by some in the African-American establishment, yet he has found open doors that otherwise might not have otherwise been open to him.

Jakes's approach to improving the civil rights of African-American people has differed from the approach that has been common over the last half century. Many civil rights leaders have been at the forefront of working to raise the minimum wage, increase government support for Medicaid, and create affirmative action in the areas of education and employment. While he has not opposed these efforts, Jakes has placed more emphasis on African-Americans doing what they can to raise themselves up economically through education and entrepreneurship. He develops and hosts conferences that encourage African-Americans to start businesses and seek networking opportunities with other African-Americans who are climbing up the economic ladder. He uses himself as an example of how God can bless someone who employs hard work, responsibility, faithfulness, and wise business methods.

> Jakes's approach to improving civil rights is to place more emphasis on African-Americans doing what they can to raise themselves up economically.

Yet Jakes also published a commentary entitled "The New Face of Affirmative Action" in which he discussed in detail his opinion on the issue. He wrote that decisions by the Supreme Court, as well as policy decisions made by the Bush Administration's Department of Education, have impacted affirmative action more than any other factors in nearly a half century. Jakes quoted the famous and revered speech of the late Dr. Martin Luther King: "I have a dream that my four children will one day live in a nation where they will not be judged by the color of their skin, but by the content of their character." He wrote that despite the achievements in racial equality over the last forty years, the country had still not achieved Dr. King's vision. It would be a great thing if the country were indeed color-blind, but that time has not yet come. As long as there are inequalities in the quality of basic education as well as higher education, steps must be taken to level the playing field. He compared the situation to giving one man a spoon and another a shovel and asking them both to dig a hole. He concluded by quoting from the book of Joel,

> So I will restore to you the years that the swarming locust has eaten, the crawling locust, the consuming locust, and the chewing locust, my great army which I sent among you. (Joel 2:25)

Jakes said that restoration is only completed when it is proportionate to the damage done.

Many prominent civil rights leaders have acknowledged T. D.'s rising stature among the African-American community. In the days after Hurricane Katrina, he met with Operation PUSH's Jesse Jackson, the National Urban League's Marc Morial, the NAACP's Bruce Gordon, the Congressional Black Caucus' Mel Watt, and congresswoman Sheila Jackson Lee of Texas. A few days after these meetings, longtime civil rights leader and former presidential candidate Jesse Jackson released a statement about his relationship with Jakes. Jackson spoke of meeting with him at former President Clinton's three-day Global Initiative Conference just after Katrina. Jackson spoke of the widespread attitude that the response to Katrina was not as prompt or intense as it could have been.

> Once the issue of race got out there, [Bush] started reaching out for blacks he knew to stand with him to offset criticism basically coming from the media itself. I believe that Bishop Jakes is pushing him.[81]

Jakes does not ignore the country's racial problems, but he sees racism as more than a social issue; he sees it as a spiritual problem. He defines racism as what it is: sin. In a message at a church near Cincinnati, he instructed his primarily white audience in how to deal with racism.

We must preach against racism. Add racism to your list of sins. Preach it in your neighborhoods. Preach it in the suburbs, until people are convicted and they're falling on the altar and confessing racist behavior. Go ahead and preach against abortion. But when you get through preaching against abortion, give us some milk up in here, so that we can feed the babies you told us we ought to have.[82]

Although Jakes has been a frequent guest of the White House, whether it is occupied by Democrats or Republicans, he does not shy away from discussing politics and political issues. He prefers to call everyone to account: Democrats and Republicans, as well as African-Americans involved in the political process.

African-Americans are making grave mistakes in allowing themselves to be controlled or owned by a particular political party. I think that when it is presumed that we're going to vote a particular way, frankly, the Democratic Party takes us for granted because they feel like they own us. And the Republican Party fails to provide the things that would draw us because they feel like they can't get us. And I think we need to approach the politics from a non-partisan posture and make the parties fight for our allegiance by coming up with agendas that are of interest to people of color.[83]

Just before the crucial mid-term elections of 2006, Jakes issued a statement encouraging African-Americans to consider issues and not just parties when marking the ballot.

Members of the black clergy face a challenge in the upcoming political season to refrain from being used by any political party or ideological agenda to further their aims at the expense of the critical issues facing our communities. As we approach the midterm congressional elections, poverty—at home and abroad—economic and educational parity—or the lack there-of—voting rights and accessibility; reconstruction of the Gulf Coast; and the war in Iraq are all critical issues that African-Americans should consider as we head to the ballet box.[84]

MOST INFLUENTIAL

Ministries Today magazine listed the "Top 20 Influencers" in its January/February 2003 issue. This was strictly a list of those who were influencing the Pentecostal and charismatic movements in the postmodern era. T. D. Jakes was first on the list, cited before such notables as Benny Hinn, Kenneth Copeland, Pat Robertson, Joel Osteen, and John Hagee. Some of these men have been active in these movements for over twenty years. Having been in national ministry for less than a decade, T. D. Jakes has truly emerged.

The Church Report published its list of "The 50 Most Influential Christians in America" in January 2006. As in previous years, the list named people from various backgrounds across the American Christian landscape. One thing that made this list different was that, for the first time, an African-American headed a list that included individuals of many ethnicities and backgrounds. Bishop T. D. Jakes was listed as the most influential Christian in America. When told of the honor, Jakes said he was really flabbergasted to be honored in this way. He was listed above the likes of Joel Osteen, Rick Warren, Bill Hybels, and even legendary evangelist Billy Graham. Whether one agrees with him or not, or likes him or not, it cannot be argued anymore that former hillbilly preacher T. D. Jakes is a national Christian leader.

> Jakes does not ignore the country's racial problems, but he sees racism as more than a social issue; he sees it as a spiritual problem.

7

FAMILY LIFE

God uses ordinary people and I think my secret is my
ordinariness. I consider myself to be very ordinary in a
very extraordinary world.

—T. D. Jakes[85]

Chapter Seven

FAMILY LIFE

T. D. Jakes is a family man. He has worked tirelessly his entire life to provide for his wife and children. Jakes watched his father work hard for years to provide for his family and then watched as it all went away because of illness. The lessons of those years have had an impact upon his life that has never gone away.

From the time they became a couple, even before they were married, Jakes strived to take care of Serita as well as he could. On the first Christmas they spent together, he convinced his mother to invite Serita and her mother to join them in their home. That day, he presented Serita with a complete outfit, including a sweater and shawl. A present like that was no small sacrifice for the young man, but it pleased Jakes to no end that he was able to take care of her in this way.

T. D. and Serita have admitted that they are opposites. T. D. is happiest when he is out in the world "flittering and fluttering," as Serita describes it. She, on the other hand, is a homebody. Instead of pulling them apart, however, their differences seem to draw them together. T. D. says, "We complement each other....We give each other what the other wants and needs; we build each other up in the places where we are broken."[86]

For the celebration of his fiftieth birthday, Jakes wrote a tribute to Serita for the way she has supported him through the years.

When I had holes in my shoes and no electricity, you were there to support me and the ministry. The investment didn't look as promising back then. It seems like now that I've made it, it's over. But I'm still doing this because I feel obligated. I owe it to them, those who supported my early years, and I give thanks to them....I'm doing this because I think there might be another me out there in the pews.

My wife has been around over half of my life, and it's funny how I can remember the exact spot in her mother's house where I knew that she was going to be my wife. It's not only her feminine persona or the grace by which she walks, but it's that in twenty-five years she never disrespected me, and she never complained.

There were times when the lights were out and we had no gas. Speaking engagements would raise an offering for me and my family and I would give the money to someone else that needed it. Our very own members would have to pick us up to go to church and sometimes I would travel 500 miles to preach to five people. She always supported me. I am 100 percent positive that I would not have made it in ministry without her.[87]

STARTING A FAMILY

The birth of the first child in a family is a life-changing experience. When the first birth is a multiple birth, the impact is even more life-changing. T. D. and Serita welcomed twin boys, Jermaine and Jamar, into the world in 1980. They were born twenty-eight minutes apart, an unusually long period for twin boys.

When they were born, things in the Jakes household were relatively secure with T. D. working at Union Carbide. T. D. and Serita were still very young when T. D. lost the job and the difficult years began. In 1987, a daughter, Cora, was born, followed by her sister, Sarah, a year later. By this time, T. D.'s church was beginning to grow and the family was able to move up from absolute poverty to what might be termed the lower class.

In 1992, the family took the huge risk of using the money they had saved for a down payment on a new home to self-publish T. D.'s first book. By 1993, the Jakes family was able to afford a new home. They later purchased one of the best known, and most expensive, homes in Charleston—not the run-of-the-mill pastor's residence in West Virginia. Thus, it became the talk of the town and front page news in their community.

Another year of change hit the Jakes family in 1995 when they not only moved to Dallas, but also welcomed the addition of their youngest child, Thomas Dexter Jakes Jr., whom they would refer to as Dexter. It was almost as if T. D. and Serita had three different families. The twin boys were fifteen and dealing with the teen struggles of high school. The girls were seven and eight and experiencing the early stages of adolescence. And with Dexter, they were back to diapers once again.

> Jakes watched his father work hard for years to provide for his family, and then watched as it all went away.

The move to Dallas created headlines for the Jakes family once again. The home they purchased was a 9,689-square-foot mansion located around the corner from wealthy oil industry magnates. What was not well-known at the time was that they had not yet sold the house in West Virginia. The top end of the market in Charleston was much softer than Jakes had realized, so for over a year they maintained the operating costs of two very large and expensive homes.

A few years later, the Jakes family moved to a different home, this time in Fort Worth. This home is even larger than the first home. Located in east Fort Worth, it is around 12,000 square feet on seventeen acres of land and is reported to have cost 5.2 million dollars. By most standards, it is considered an estate. According to Tarrant County records, the house has four bedrooms, five baths, and a six-car garage. Some time after they bought the home, a spokesman for Jakes, Mark Demoss, told the media that T. D. and Serita moved to Fort Worth "specifically for more privacy and safety, particularly given that he travels a lot and has a wife and children."[88] In 2006, Jakes revealed in a sermon that natural gas was found in the ground beneath his home just a few months after he purchased it. As the owner of the largest parcel of land in the area, he received the greatest amount of royalties from the company that discovered and drilled the gas well.

JACQUELINE

Jakes's older sister, Jacqueline, had always been supportive of her little brother's ministry, but she quickly became an integral part of The Potter's House. Jacqueline had left home not long after she graduated from high school at the age of seventeen, bound for Washington, D.C., to start her adult life. At twenty-nine, she suffered a brain tumor and spent the next ten years fighting for her life with risky surgery that left her paralyzed on one side of her body. Radiation treatments then took away her peripheral vision. By this time, Jacqueline was a single mother going through some of the most demanding challenges one could imagine. At times, she and her daughter were on food stamps and didn't know how they would survive. Because this was before T. D. experienced his financial breakthrough, he was unable to provide any financial support during her time of need. Odith, however, became an even stronger prayer warrior during her daughter's health journey. She implored the Lord to reach out and touch Jacqueline. T. D. would later write of how impressed he was by the fervent prayers of his mother.[89]

Eventually, Jacqueline made a complete recovery, and today she is on staff at The Potter's House. She has authored several books and regularly speaks to women, encouraging them to keep their faith in the Lord strong regardless of the trials they experience.

ERNEST JAKES JR.

T. D.'s brother, Ernest Jakes Jr., has also been supportive of his younger brother's ministry throughout the years. Though not nearly as public as his sister is or as his late mother was, Ernest has nevertheless been by T. D.'s side whenever needed. Even though he is several years older than his brother, Ernest has been a friend and confidant as he, too, strives to touch the world for the Lord.

VIRGINIA JAMISON

The mothers of T. D. and Serita have played major roles throughout their children's lives. Both lived to see the ministerial success that their children were able to experience. Virginia Jamison, Serita's mother, was very supportive of the ministry and her son-in-law in particular. She believed that T. D. could do anything he set his mind to do, and she never let him forget that. Far from a fair-weather believer, she had been there for the difficult times in West Virginia when food and money were scarce. Again, she would often provide meals to make certain the twins were well-nourished. When Christmases were tight, Virginia came with sacks of gifts for everyone and a Christmas dinner to provide some holiday spirit.

She remained a great support in Dallas as the ministry began to grow and thrive. While T. D. always had a "mama" in Odith, he affectionately referred to Virginia as "Mother." Not long after the move to Dallas, Virginia became critically ill. As the family gathered at her side, they were informed that the situation was grave. At first, Virginia seemed to rally, causing everyone to wonder if perhaps the doctors were incorrect. She smiled at jokes even though she was hooked up to a myriad of medical equipment that kept her heart beating and her lungs working. T. D. brought Odith to see her, as well, since they had become good friends over the years. Odith Jakes was not in the best of health herself, but as she walked into the room of the ailing woman and saw her surrounded by all of her children and grandchildren, she spoke words that reflected the faith of both women: "You must be a happy woman! You got all your children gathered around your bed."[90] T. D. was somewhat taken aback by his mother's words, but Virginia smiled and nodded in agreement.

Their optimism proved to be short lived. The next day Virginia took a turn for the worse and fell into unconsciousness, and the family was told that it was time to say good-bye. They surrounded her bed and tried to will her healing with the power of their love, but she slipped away into the arms of her Lord. Serita cried and whispered, "My mother is gone."[91]

ODITH JAKES

It was not too many months later that T. D. experienced the same loss. Odith had been his greatest supporter since he was a child. Their shared experience of going through the illness and death of Ernest Jakes Sr. had a strong impact upon their relationship. When T. D. had preached in that first storefront church, his mother had been there supporting him. During the years of struggle after he had been laid off from Union Carbide, she had been there for him in every way she could. When he'd moved from West Virginia to Dallas, she had supported him in the move and lived to see her son become a national religious celebrity.

Jakes has often written about how his mother taught him to pray. He describes her prayers during Jacqueline's illness in this way:

Let me tell you, nobody can pray like a mama whose baby is deathly ill—even when her baby is an adult. I had never heard anybody pray the way my mother prayed when my sister was sick. I had heard plenty of people pray, but never like this. She would not back down, she would not let down, she would not calm down. She would not get up and she would not shut up as she literally bombarded heaven on my sister's behalf. She became a warrior far superior to any epic hero. She became a giant on her knees. With a sword in one hand she battled the enemies of death and disease, and with her other hand stretched toward heaven she kept beseeching God's help and His mercy.[92]

T. D.'s life was moving at lightning speed when he received the news that his mother had become seriously ill. He stopped everything to go to her side. He wanted the best doctors, the best treatment, and the best hospitals. The diagnosis was a brain tumor. Slowly, this great lady who had taught hundreds of students, as well as her own children, became unable to remember many of the things she had taught. Over a period of nearly a year, she would have eight surgeries. The disease would ravage her body for more than two years before it would take her life.

> After the death of his mother, Serita encouraged T. D. to spend time with men who were not afraid to show their grief in front of others. He took her advice.

Even during this difficult time, Odith remained a rock of strength for T. D. and the rest of her family. Her spirit remained strong to the end, even as her body grew increasingly frail and her mind lost its clarity. Toward the end, she had a hard time distinguishing between T. D. and his older brother, Ernest Jr. At one point, a frustrated T. D. said to her, "I don't see how you are handling this!" His mother reassured him, "You do what you have to do, and don't you forget it!"[93] Odith P. Jakes died on August 16, 1999.

The time following his mother's death was challenging for T. D. He had to resume his busy schedule almost immediately after the funeral. He had commitments that simply could not be broken, but he continued to grieve the loss.

Serita would later write of his deep grief. In *Beside Every Good Man*, Serita wrote that T. D. felt that he was being weak when he allowed his grief to show in front of his wife. She felt he needed to be with other men who had experienced the loss of their mothers. She encouraged him to spend time with men who were not afraid to show their grief in front of others. He took her advice.

THE JAKES CHILDREN

In December 2004, T. D.'s son, Jamar, suffered two heart attacks at the tender age of twenty-four. Jakes cancelled a sermon in Nigeria and rushed home to help him recover. Later, he spoke about this experience, saying, "Above everything we do in ministry, our first call is to our own family. My only wish was for my son to come home. He was all that I wanted for Christmas."[94] Fortunately, Jamar recovered and continues to do well under the care of doctors.

Today, Jamar works with the Conference Department at The Potter's House. He was one of the main planners involved with the Mega Youth Experience during the Atlanta MegaFest Conferences. Jamar describes his mission in life in this way: "My mission is to be the voice and the hand that encourages people to change their lives through hope, comfort, and peace."[95] Jamar also describes growing up learning the fundamentals of business. "Working behind the scenes in most of my father's companies allowed me a panoramic view of both business and finance."[96]

Jermaine, the Jakes's youngest twin, is interested in music. He is a part of Dexterity Sound, T. D.'s recording label, where he has been involved in new artist development. One of his new discoveries is Lewis Banks Jr., also known as Grenade, an evangelist and urban entertainer. When Jermaine saw Banks' first video, he got in touch with the artist and suggested they get together. Within a few weeks, Banks was performing at the 2006 MegaFest Conference in front of thousands of young people. Jermaine has also been the master of ceremonies for various awards shows and concerts in Dallas and around the country. With numerous CDs being released by Dexterity Sound, both within The Potter's House family and beyond, Jermaine has no problem staying busy.

Cora is the older of T. D.'s two girls. She has received many of her father's attributes. She seems to be a leader among young people. She has also acknowledged the call of God on her life. T. D. has acknowledged this call as well.

> My oldest daughter, Cora, has just acknowledged her call to the ministry, and I'm really proud about that. We didn't push her or coerce her, but under her own self-evaluation and digging down into her own spirit, she sensed the voice of God calling her into ministry. Her passion is ministering to teenagers and people her own age.[97]

Sarah, the Jakes's youngest daughter, graduated from high school a year early because of her academic achievements. She is currently majoring in business at a nearby university and shows signs of the same thirst for knowledge that her grandmother Odith had. She also described the business education she received growing up:

> Fortunately, I know that no matter how much money you have, you must budget—whether it's $10,000 or $1,000,000. I believe that I have been able to budget effectively because of the business transactions I have seen up close....Most people my age cannot say that they understand the pros and cons of a 401(k), or stocks and bonds, but because of my willingness to learn about my father's business transactions, I have benefited immensely.[98]

Young Thomas Dexter was born in the days after *Woman, Thou Art Loosed!* and does not remember the early days of poverty. He has been raised in big houses without any memory of being in need. He is the one whom his father speaks about most from the pulpit. T. D. often tells of something that Dexter did or said and then jokingly pleads with the congregation to keep it a secret.

There is one more member of the family. Malachi is the grandson who came out of season. T. D. and Serita had to examine themselves when they discovered that their fourteen-year-old daughter was pregnant. This was especially troubling for T. D., who had long been counseling and offering guidance to young women. At first, Jakes kept the situation hidden, perhaps out of fear for his own reputation if it were to appear to some that the preacher was unable to keep his own house in order. It is more likely, however, that he was acting as a father protecting his young daughter in crisis from the harsh glare of the public eye.

There was good reason for his caution. A local reporter going through the Jakes's trash dug up the truth along with the daughter's medical records. When it was brought into the open, the family simply acknowledged the situation and handled it as the private family matter that it was. They did not shame their daughter but stood beside her. To this day, Jakes has not acknowledged which of his two daughters is Malachi's mother. When asked about the unexpected birth of his grandson, he declined to discuss the matter publicly other than to say, "Our church is not based upon me presenting myself as this flawless, invincible hero who's never been through anything. But details to me are the last remaining shreds of private life that I can offer my children."[99]

T. D. enthusiastically plays the role of proud grandpa these days. In 2006, it was Malachi who helped the entire family kick off MegaFest 2006. The *Atlanta Journal-Constitution* reported on the moment.

> "I'm a grandpa now," Jakes said. "Everybody say, 'PaPa.'" Jakes's children bantered with the crowd, then Jakes handed the microphone to his grandson, Malachi, a toddler who clung to his big leg for protection. Malachi then found his preaching voice: 'Welcome, welcome to Mega...' But he gave up because he couldn't say

the word, MegaFest. Smiling, Jakes took the microphone as the crowd cooed at the shy boy. For once, Jakes was upstaged.[100]

Much like movie stars, sports figures, and national politicians, T. D. and Serita Jakes have had to carefully navigate the fine line between being public figures and private citizens. Decisions had to be made regarding what information was for public consumption—and sermon illustration—and what was to be withheld. The Jakes's children, and now their grandchild, did not bargain for growing up in the harsh glare of media attention and public speculation. Most families would be mortified if their children's every movement, mistake, and milestone ended up in the newspaper the next day. Indeed, the world of the Jakes children has turned out to be very different from the one that T. D. and Serita knew when they were growing up. Like all parents, they made the calls they felt they had to make regarding their children. Those decisions may not have all been correct or popular ones, but T. D. and Serita have preserved their family's health and unity the best way they knew how.

THE NEW MEDIA MOGUL

You couldn't say Santa Barbara was the target audience
for this film, but white women stood up and said,
"Thank you for telling my story."

—Reuben Cannon
Woman, Thou Art Loosed movie producer[101]

Chapter Eight

THE NEW MEDIA MOGUL

From the very beginning of his ministry, T. D. Jakes showed a penchant for using every available method to communicate the gospel and the limitless love of God. From demonstrative preaching to music production to women's Sunday school classes to books and even dramatic plays, Jakes's "outside the box" methodology has continued, even in the face of criticism. In an interview, Jakes firmly stated,

> I understand the importance of drama and storytelling. I think they bring an important perspective to ministry, and for me this is harmonious with preaching. As preachers, we are engaged in storytelling every Sunday, sharing the story of the Good News of who Christ is, and dramatizing those words so people can experience them.[102]

T. D. Jakes remains every bit as much a businessman as he is a preacher. Growing up in poverty-stricken West Virginia, Jakes knew the plight of the poor. He knew that the answer wasn't to be found in waiting for or existing on government handouts. The things Jakes learned as a child, watching his father build a business with a mop and a bucket and his mother invest in real estate, have been put to good use in his life today. Jakes has never been one to shy away from combining religion and business, as he made clear in a CNN interview:

You know, I do understand business. I grew up in a house of entrepreneurs. I own several companies myself, but there's a difference between what you do and who you are. When it comes to my faith, it embraces whose I am, but business is what I do. And I think that there's a great appreciation, a cross-pollination, because if we are going to affect people who do business, we have to do business with them. And as a Christian, I love to do that, because my faith bleeds over in how I handle business. Ethics are appropriate in business.[103]

T. D. has always been a goal-oriented person. In the early pages of his first book, Jakes challenged women to write down thirty things they would like to do with their lives and to cross them off as they were accomplished.[104] No doubt, Jakes has his own list of things he wishes to accomplish before he dies.

As stated earlier, not long after publishing *Woman, Thou Art Loosed!* Jakes created the limited liability corporation T. D. Jakes Enterprises to produce all subsequent books and to investigate the use of other media in order to reach out to mainstream audiences across America. TDJE has its own facility, employees, bank accounts, and board of directors. As a church, The Potter's House hosts various conferences and meetings using its staff and facilities. TDJE now conducts various conferences and meetings and often hosts them in facilities away from the church, sometimes in the Dallas area but often in other cities around the country.

PUBLISHING

Today, with over thirty books to his credit, Jakes is one of the most prolific and successful writers in the country. Since the 1993 release of *Woman, Thou Art Loosed!* Jakes has released anywhere from one to four books, fiction and nonfiction, each year. Several of his books have reached the *New York Times* Best-Seller Lists. In addition to *Woman,*

Thou Art Loosed! Jakes's book *Maximize the Moment* peaked at number three on the *Times'* business best-sellers list, while *God's Leading Lady* rose to number four on the general list.

Jakes's books were initially sold at his conferences and on television, and also served as "giveaways" for financial supporters, often called "partners," who contributed regularly, often monthly, to cover the cost of the ministry's airtime and production expenses. From 1995 through 1997, Jakes released fourteen books—that's a new book about every seventy-five days for three years. In the midst of all this writing, Jakes was also moving his entire ministry and family from West Virginia to Dallas, where his notoriety exploded. Thousands of people were now coming to the church, while tens of thousands tuned in on television, and his books were flying off the shelves as fast as they were written.

> Jakes is intentional about addressing different demographics with his books. He writes on men's issues, women's issues, and business issues.

By 1998, his books were published by Putnam Books, which was doing a great deal of the publicity as Jakes continued to gain the attention of the publishing industry. No longer was he selling books only in the back of the auditorium after speaking engagements; now his books were also appearing in major bookstores, both religious and secular, around the country such as Barnes and Noble, Borders, Wal-Mart, Target, Sam's Club, and Costco.

Jakes is intentional about addressing different demographics with his books. He writes books on men's issues, women's issues, and business issues. He has produced supporting materials for some of his books, such as workbooks, group studies, and devotionals. In 2003, a study Bible was published in conjunction with the *Woman, Thou Art Loosed!* theme.

DRAMATIC PRODUCTIONS

In 1999, TDJ Enterprises produced its first play, a theatrical version of *Woman, Thou Art Loosed!* It was performed for church audiences around the country, who received it enthusiastically. In 2001, the play was broadcast to more than 80 percent of the world, with a potential audience of 5.2 billion people.

The following year, another play, *Behind Closed Doors*, was produced. It was cowritten by Jakes and Tyler Perry. The play was a close look at breast cancer and its effect on marriages. It featured the story of Mrs. Rushmore's mastectomy, an operation that saved her life but took away her confidence and self-respect. Eventually her husband fell prey to another married woman. Not to be defeated, Mrs. Rushmore picked herself up and began to fight to hold onto her man. The play toured the country to sold-out audiences.

A third production, *Cover Girls*, starring former *Facts of Life* star Kim Fields, was produced by Matthew Knowles, the father of music superstar Beyonce Knowles. The play toured twenty-eight cities across the country and played to sold-out houses and wide acclaim. It was the adaptation of a T. D. Jakes novel that told the story of four women who seemingly had nothing in common, yet each day faced the complex realities of twenty-first century urban life as they tried to balance their needs with their belief in God.

All of Jakes's plays were primarily marketed through African-American churches in the communities where they were presented. This type of marketing has been a long-standing tradition in the black community. Jakes later said, "The Gospel-play industry always invites the ministers out, giving them tickets to the plays. We've always marketed like that because we don't have the money to do it any other way."[105]

HOLLYWOOD

In 2004, *Woman, Thou Art Loosed* was produced as a theatrical film. At the time of the film's release, Jakes explained his desire to take on the project:

> I'd wanted to reenter the conversation because I learned more about these issues after I wrote the book than I'd known before, because so many people wrote me with their stories. This movie is dedicated to all of those stories. There are slices of all of them here.
>
> The response to the play was overwhelming. Many times, we would need to stop a scene and wait for the audience because they began to pray or to worship during the performance. Eventually, we started doing altar calls.
>
> As we saw that response, we began to talk about maybe doing something with video. I started dreaming. Stan Foster, a fantastic scriptwriter, started putting it together. Things started to develop. I was also amazed by the number of actors and actresses who didn't mind that we didn't have much money to offer, because they were so hungry to do something positive.[106]

The movie, produced in partnership with Reuben Cannon Productions, was shot in an amazing twelve days. It is still a rare thing in Hollywood for a film to be produced by African-Americans and to feature nearly all African-American actors. Jakes attracted several investors for the film, distributing the potential loss as well as profit. Among the investors were Oprah Winfrey, attorney Johnnie Cochran, Cedric the Entertainer, and Danny Glover. Despite the fact that the movie was generally viewed as an African-American film, Jakes proclaimed that it was for people from every background and ethnicity. "This message is for everyone. This problem is everywhere."[107]

The film was directed by Michael Schultz, best known for films he directed in the 1970s including *Which Way Is Up?* with Richard Prior and *Sgt. Pepper's Lonely Hearts Club Band*. He was also a veteran television director, including episodes for programs such as *Everwood*, *Boston Public*, *Felicity*, and *Ally McBeal*. Even though he was one of the first African-American directors to penetrate mainstream Hollywood, this was his first film in thirteen years.

Among the many things that made this movie different from most religiously based films, as well as more controversial, was its R rating. Religious critics who were unhappy with the movie's rating were even more disturbed that parts of the film were shot in a church. Jakes's movie, however, was never intended as a "family film." It dealt with the same difficult issues that Jakes tackled in his book: the abyss of prison, prostitution, and drug addiction.

> The movie *Woman, Thou Art Loosed* deals with the same difficult issues that Jakes tackled in his book: the abyss of prison, prostitution, and drug addiction.

It was the story of a woman whose rape at the tender age of twelve led her into a self-destructive lifestyle in which she worked as a stripper, became a drug addict, and eventually shot her mother's husband. T. D. made his acting debut in the film, playing himself visiting the main character while she was incarcerated.

The *Fort Worth Star Telegram* stated,

> Although some in the audience may object to the graphic scenes, Jakes says the Bible, too, is filled with R-rated stories, such as Amnon raping his half-sister, Tamar; David committing adultery with Bathsheba; and the incest between Lot and his daughters.[108]

This did not mean Jakes was pleased by the rating. He had hoped the film could be viewed by younger viewers, remarking, "I am not happy with the R-rating. The damage to these young souls starts early and there is often a family history, a generational vulnerability to abuse."[109]

In an interview with *Christianity Today*, Jakes also stated,

The film deals with difficult subject matter and does include some violence. I felt a responsibility to be true to the audience. You cannot sugarcoat child abuse. You can't make that light, and I think that's part of the ministry.

When a child has been abused, counselors often give them dolls to help them talk about it because sometimes it's easier for them to say what happened to the doll than it is to say *this happened to me*. See the movie as a doll. It's not appropriate for little children, but a teenager may be able to point to the character of Michelle and say *that happened to me*.[110]

Despite the rating, on opening weekend the movie ranked seventh in ticket sales nationally, earning $2.3 million. By the end of its second week, it had earned over five million dollars. It was the winner of the American Spirit Award at the 2004 Santa Barbara Independent Film Festival. Actresses from the film, Kimberly Elise and Loretta Devine, were nominated for Independent Spirit Awards. The film was then honored at the American Black Film Festival in Miami and was named one of the ten best films of 2004 by the United States Conference of Catholic Bishops' Office for Film and Broadcasting. After its theatrical release, the movie sold more than a million copies nationwide as a DVD.

The problem of sexual abuse and molestation is one that has become more and more prevalent, touching every segment of society—rich and poor, black and white, religious and nonreligious. The Roman Catholic Church has spent billions of dollars trying to make amends for the abuse their priests have inflicted on children. But the problem is not only with the Catholic Church. Television icon Oprah Winfrey has made no secret of the abuse that she suffered as a child. Robin Stone, former editor of *Essence* magazine, wrote a book entitled *No Secrets, No Lies*, in which she detailed her sexual abuse at the age of nine. Even as this issue is often swept under the rug of the public consciousness, T. D. Jakes and other prominent African-American pastors and leaders have worked to get this issue out into the open. By producing the book, play, and movie, Jakes wanted to let women know that sexual and physical abuse was not their fault, and it was not the end of their lives.

Many of the major newspapers and secular magazines printed reviews of the film, which almost always included at least some mention of the ministry of T. D. Jakes. *Washington Post* movie reviewer Donna Britt wrote,

> What struck me most about "Loosed"—which, in the tradition of a certain type of black theater, is broad, frank, and accessible—is its setting. It's an urban community in which the local Pentecostal church is a haven for a (mostly) committed flock that, as star Elise said, "like in real churches, shows true religious commitment and hypocrisy in the same congregation."[111]

The reporter went on to mention Jakes himself: "If you thought, 'Who?' take my word for it, the guy is huge."[112]

The *New York Times* compared it to another religious cinematic phenomenon:

> No question that religion has a powerful hold on the cultural consciousness these days. But these two films, while sold by a similar strategy, offer very different visions of Christianity. "The Passion of the Christ," an interpretation of the Gospels—however gritty, however controversial—was still a Bible story. "Woman, Thou Art Loosed," the story of a woman raped as a girl by her mother's boyfriend and the subsequent effects on her life, is a contemporary morality play told with old-fashioned Hollywood realism.[113]

Vanessa E. Jones of the *Boston Globe* wrote about T. D.'s promotion of the film.

> During a summer trek that stopped in Chicago, Atlanta, New York, and other cities, Jakes whipped up interest by showing the film not only to religious leaders but to counselors, psychologists, and advocates toiling in the area of abuse. He capped the marketing blitz with an hour-long appearance on "Oprah" on Oct. 1—the day "Woman Thou Art Loosed" premiered in 408 theaters nationally.[114]

Many other national newspapers and magazines reviewed or made note of the film, including *USA Today* and *People* magazine. Some called the film "trite" and "preachy," but no matter their words, it was the kind of publicity that could not have been purchased at any price.

TDJ Enterprises set a release date of September 2008 for the film adaptation of his novel *Not Easily Broken*. Under the direction of veteran Hollywood actor and director Bill Duke, the film stars Morris Chestnut and Taraji Henson as a "couple whose marriage is pulled to the breaking point in their struggle to balance faith, family, and finances in a real life setting."[115]

It certainly seems that Jakes's intentions are to make films a permanent part of his effort to communicate the gospel. Films also allow him to address difficult issues in a medium where they are more easily received by all kinds of people. There are those, of course, who have a hard time accepting this. There are segments of the Pentecostal denomination, including those whom Jakes associated with early in his ministry, who regard all movies as offensive. They would never encourage parishioners to attend a film in a movie theater. Nevertheless, in a culture where a vast majority of the population subscribe to cable television and own DVD players, movies have penetrated our society. Like any other medium, film can either be used as a tool to reach people for Jesus Christ or it can be used by the enemy to further capture their souls.

Music

Although his ministry for the last twenty years has not centered around music, Jakes is still talented in this area and he knows what will touch the hearts and minds of people. He understands what it takes to make quality music and accepts nothing less in the projects he undertakes.

For the *Woman, Thou Art Loosed!* CD, Jakes introduced the story-line using his singing voice as well as his preaching skills. Then, the message of how women do not need to feel bound by the circumstances of their lives was told in song by some of the best voices in the industry, including Vickie Winans and Shirley Caesar. The CD was nominated for both Dove and Grammy awards.

> Jakes wanted to let women know that sexual and physical abuse was not their fault, and it was not the end of their lives.

Jakes later created a music label, Dexterity Sounds, producing numerous albums that have sold in the millions. The label was created in collaboration with EMI Gospel. Of the first eight albums Dexterity produced, five received Grammy nominations. The album *A Wing and a Prayer*, featuring Jakes and The Potter's House Choir, received the 2004 Grammy Award for "Best Gospel Choir or Chorus Album." The award was accepted by choir director Steve Lawrence and Jamar Jakes. T. D. was unable to attend because the award ceremony was held on a Sunday evening, and he was preaching. After the ceremony, Jakes released a statement of thanks and appreciation: "The main reason that we release albums is to spread the Word of God through music. We are honored to receive a Grammy, which I'm sure will help us touch more lives."[116]

This is the same man who, as a child, asked for a piano as a Christmas present. This is the same man who began his career as a music minister in a small, rural church. He was now producing award-winning gospel music for the world. Many of the recording projects also include segments of Jakes's preaching. The album *T.D. Jakes Presents God's Leading Ladies* features some of the most prominent African-American performers, including Patti LaBelle, Stacie Orrico, and four members of the Winans family, as well as a two-minute sermon from Jakes about Mary Magdalene.

Jakes often takes part in other musical projects, such as Kirk Franklin's 2002 album, *The Rebirth of Kirk Franklin*, for which T. D. performed a piece with Franklin about the 9/11 terrorist attacks. Franklin presents himself as someone who comes to Jakes deeply troubled by the attacks. T. D. responds with words of wisdom and comfort. Franklin and T. D. then speak back and forth surrounded by the musical accompaniment. The album was a mixture of rap, drama, and a moving sermon. It received the 2003 Dove Award for "Contemporary Gospel Album of the Year."

Another example of the musical respect Jakes has garnered is his invitation to participate in a project with award-winning Christian musician and songwriter, Bill Gaither. Gaither is perhaps the most respected Christian songwriter in the Southern Gospel genre. Together, they created an album entitled *The Bridge*, recorded live at The Potter's House as a celebration of cultural and ethnic diversity.

In interviews interspersed between the songs and in the bonus materials, Jakes described the role that music has played in his ministry. He spoke of leading the choir in the Baptist church when he was a boy and how explaining the message of the songs to the choir helped him to develop skills that would later serve him well in his preaching.

T. D.'s musical projects have all maintained a standard of excellence that has been recognized by both Christian and secular musical organizations. In 2003, two albums, *Follow the Star* and *A Wing and a Prayer*, were nominated for Grammy Awards. If T. D. Jakes did not pastor a church, preach sermons, or write books, he would still be one of the most celebrated musicians and music producers in the country today.

ALTERNATIVE MEDIA

In addition to books, plays, movies, and music, TDJ Enterprises is also developing articles, educational opportunities, sermons, and programming for radio as well as the Internet. One of the newest additions is The Bishop's Blog,[117] which allows Jakes to comment on an array of topics relevant to the culture, as well as to inform people about his current schedule.

TDJ Enterprises also produces a variety of greeting cards in conjunction with Hallmark. Executives from the card company attended the 2000 Woman, Thou Art Loosed! conference and shortly thereafter reached an agreement with TDJ Enterprises to develop a "Loose Your Spirit: Messages of Faith and Inspiration" line.

> Films allow Jakes to address difficult issues in a medium where they are more easily received by all kinds of people.

In partnership with Jay Sekulow of the American Center for Law and Justice, TDJ Enterprises purchased Lifeline Communications and Affinity Marketing, renaming it Affinity4. The new company offers telecom services, call centers, insurance, and other products, all with a 10 percent "giveback" to charities and ministries of the customer's choosing. Over the last decade, Affinity4 has provided over $75 million in contributions to charities and ministries.

T. D. Jakes has continually crossed and merged the boundaries between church, ministry, entertainment, and business, and he has done so, for the most part, without compromising his message or his integrity. He has formed relationships with pastors, celebrities, politicians, and athletes in ways that have helped all involved. Perhaps *Publisher's*

Weekly religion editor Phyllis Tickle said it best in an interview she gave to *Christianity Today*: "There seems to be in T. D. Jakes's body of thought something that bridges ethnic [and denominational] differences. That he has managed to do that with commercial success is very significant."[118]

NATIONAL CONFERENCES

We're building on good news and blasting at the bad.
We're doing it with essential knowledge wrapped in real
lives of the best of a generation. Changes come as we
take mentoring to a new level.

—T. D. Jakes[119]

Chapter Nine

NATIONAL CONFERENCES

I n 1983, as mentioned before, T. D. Jakes held his first conference, Back to the Bible. It was geared for pastors and church leaders and attracted around eighty people. At the time, T. D. was not yet thirty years old and was struggling to keep things together financially, both at home and at his church. Within a decade, this conference would be attracting people from twenty states as well as Canada and Africa.

WTAL

After the publication of *Woman, Thou Art Loosed!* in 1993, Jakes began to hold WTAL conferences. By 1994, he was hosting twenty such conferences in cities across the country. In 1996, the decision was made to make WTAL conferences an annual event held in a designated city. Holding numerous conferences all over the nation while maintaining the television ministry and overseeing the growth of The Potter's House had become a bit too much to handle. The first national WTAL conference was conducted in New Orleans in 1997. New Orleans had become practically a second home to Jakes and the ministry because of local friends such as Bishop Paul Morton and T. D.'s history with the Full Gospel Baptist Fellowship.

In 1998, twenty-two thousand women attended the national WTAL Conference in Tampa, Florida. In addition to Jakes, Juanita Bynum and Bishop Noel Jones spoke and were very well received. Through the years, the conferences have helped many women transition from the welfare track to the work world. In 1999, the conference set a national indoor attendance record for Atlanta's Georgia Dome when 84,459 women attended one service, topping the previous record for the facility that had been set by a Billy Graham crusade. Over a three-day period, 265,000 women were present at that conference.

In 2000, T. D. Jakes Enterprises announced that the conference would be renamed Woman, Thou Art Loosed Plus and would emphasize the economic empowerment of women. Jakes's vision was for it to be more than a feel-good conference where women would get a "spiritual high" for a couple of days. He wanted them to be able to go back home and deal with their real lives. He wanted them to receive pragmatic answers for everyday problems. He wanted it to be a life-changing experience, both spiritually and financially—something that would alter their lives forever.

> Each company at the event paid $2,500 to have a booth and to introduce itself to an often-ignored market demographic—African-American women.

At the 2001 conference, held again in New Orleans, representatives from businesses and government agencies were available in the exhibition area. Hibernia National Bank was there to give women information on applying for a private or business loan. The nonprofit Consumer Credit Counseling Service was there to advise women on buying a first home, dealing with real estate agents, and applying for a mortgage. State Farm Insurance was there with information on insurance needs for cars or homes. The Social Security Administration was there to help those who qualified for disability or other benefits. There were representatives from major corporations, as well from as smaller mom-and-pop companies. Each company at the event paid $2,500 to have a booth and to introduce itself to an often-ignored market demographic—African-American women.

Jakes was always looking for ways to enhance the experience of his conferences. In 2003, he worked with *Gospel Today* magazine to unveil a new supplement, "New Power Trip," with articles on breaking through glass ceilings, securing financial futures, and developing inner strengths. The magazine released the supplement to the 50,000 women present at the conference.

ManPower

Not long after he had started his WTAL conferences, Jakes knew he wanted to do something that would reach out to the men as well. As previously mentioned, in 1993, he launched the ManPower Conference to help men of all races and backgrounds address specific needs, hurts, and struggles from a biblical perspective. The goal was to encourage men to create strong marriages, to build their confidence, and to inspire them to take on responsibility in their communities. The first conference was held at Straight Street Church in Detroit, Michigan, in 1995 and had 2,500 men in attendance—twice the number that attended the *Woman, Thou Art Loosed!* conference. By 1998, Jakes was bringing Dallas Cowboys players who had been converted to the ManPower Conferences, further adding to its appeal to men across the country.

Early in the process, T. D. made the arrangements for the ManPower Conferences to be broadcast into prisons across the country. The Prison Satellite Network is a band of satellites broadcasting to more than two hundred and seventy men's and women's prisons nationally. Jakes's desire was to impact the prison community by bringing inmates into contact with the conferences, allowing them to participate in something outside of the prison walls and preparing them for their eventual release. There are more African-American men in prisons and jails than there are in institutions of higher learning. In order to make a difference in the African-American community, the needs and issues of these men must be addressed. These men were the sons, husbands, and fathers of millions of people in the African-American community. If they are ever to be able to make a difference in their families and communities on the outside, they will have to make significant changes in their lives while on the inside.

These conferences for men and women reflect the different ways in which men and women approach God, a concept Jakes addressed in his book, *So You Call Yourself a Man.*

> In the last several years, I've ministered to large groups of women and to large groups of men, and I've noticed a significant difference in the two groups. Women aren't at all reluctant to get into the trenches of spiritual warfare. I invite women to praise and worship the Lord, and then often I have to tell them when to quit so I can get on with my next point! They have no problem at all crying out to God or weeping unashamedly for the desires of their hearts—even if it means that their eye makeup goes streaming down their faces. They have no problem with raising their voices in prayer or laying on their sisters and rebuking the devil off their lives.
>
> But when I invite a group of men to enter into the warfare of praise and worship, sometimes I'm lucky to get a couple of hallelujahs. If some men stand and praise the Lord for longer than thirty seconds, they think they've sacrificed a great deal of time and energy. Even under a strong anointing, some men find it difficult to enter into a fierce spiritual battle.[120]

PROMISE KEEPERS

In the mid-1990s, Jakes became a frequent and popular speaker at Promise Keepers conferences in stadiums and arenas around the country. He urged men to be the priests of their homes, to lead their families in worship of the Lord, to be faithful to their wives, and to be examples of godliness to their children. He told them that it was okay for a man to be sensitive to the needs of his wife and children.

GOD'S LEADING LADIES

In 2002, Jakes celebrated the tenth anniversary of his Woman, Thou Art Loosed conferences. The decade had been a time of more changes in the life and ministry of T. D. Jakes than perhaps any other in his life. A new conference, God's Leading Ladies, was also conducted in conjunction with the tenth anniversary WTAL conference to help Christian women to grow spiritually and to develop their God-given leadership abilities. In 2003, Jakes announced that the God's Leading Ladies conference would travel across the country in conjunction with his new book, God's Leading Lady. The conferences were intended to bridge the divide between the secular and spiritual worlds, aiming to help African-American women deal with financial, health, and relationship issues.

The history and scope of T. D. Jakes's conferences reflect their changing purposes. In the mid-1990s, the conferences taught attendees that God loved them in spite of anything they may have done or anything that may have happened to them in their lives. They dealt with the deep emotional scars that had been created by life circumstances and events. They helped both men and women to regain self-esteem and perspective on life. They helped men to understand their role in the family and to lead their families with greater sensitivity to the needs of their wives and children.

But as time went by, Jakes began to see that this was not enough. Men and women who lived in poverty needed practical as well as spiritual help. It was not enough for them to look forward to heaven as their home; they needed help in dealing with the everyday problems of life. For example, men who find themselves unable to properly provide for their families are going to be frustrated no matter how much they love the Lord. So Jakes began to do everything possible to help the attendees grow in every facet of their lives—not just spiritually, but also relationally, vocationally, and financially.

This change in approach brought Jakes some criticism. Many leaders in the civil rights movement have traditionally focused on people receiving more and more assistance from the government in the form of an increased minimum wage and greater subsidies for housing, food, and education. While Jakes made certain that people were aware of all of the government's programs, he also wanted government help to be a stepping-stone toward their becoming prosperous and self-supporting. He wanted people to become business-savvy employers, not merely employees. He understood that people rarely become wealthy by working for someone else. Jakes desired to give people tools that could change their lives forever.

> Jakes impacted the prison community by bringing inmates into contact with his conferences, allowing them to particpate in something outside the prison walls.

Other critics took Jakes to task for moving his preaching beyond basic Christian doctrine. They believed that teaching people about buying houses, starting businesses, and building the finances of a family was outside the purview of ministry, and they wished that Jakes would instead strictly concentrate on sharing the gospel.

MEGAFEST

In 2004, Jakes combined two of his conferences into one huge event that he dubbed MegaFest. When asked how MegaFest came to be, T.D. said, "It began when we suggested to women at Woman, Thou Art Loosed that they should come together with ManPower, and they cheered and roared. We asked the men the same thing, and they cheered and roared. We had nine months to put together something that should have taken two years."[121]

MegaFest was held in Atlanta. Over a quarter of a million tickets were sold for the many events and venues featured at the conference. It was the largest event held in Atlanta since the 1996 Olympics and had an economic impact on the city estimated at over one hundred million dollars. In addition to incorporating the ManPower and Woman, Thou Art Loosed conferences, MegaFest also included the Youth 3D Experience for teens.

Among the speakers who addressed the attendees were financial guru Suze Orman, author and televangelist Joyce Meyer, and television host Paula White. There were also speakers from other walks of life, such as former NBA star Magic Johnson, comedian and television star Steve Harvey, Grammy Award-winner Patti LaBelle, African-American businessman Steadman Graham, and Judge Joe Brown. There were counseling sessions and workshops on business ethics, home buying, and health and fitness. A family expo offered everything from voter registration to beauty makeovers to artwork.

MegaFest also reached out to people around the world. The event included "talkbacks" (live dialogue) with audiences in Cape Town, South Africa; Adelaide, Australia; and Nairobi, Kenya. MegaFest events were translated into Spanish and French for attendees from over fifty countries. Portions of the event were also simulcast to over four hundred prisons around the United States. MegaFest attracted a number of corporate sponsors, such as Delta Air Lines, Coca-Cola, Bank of America, St. Joseph's Aspirin, Lincoln Mercury, MetLife Financial, The Bahamas Tourist Office, and Nextel Communications.

Jakes stated his intentions for the huge event,

I hope that people will go away from MegaFest understanding that Christians are multi-dimensional. That we're not just churchy, that we don't just worship. That's part of what we do, but we also laugh and we interact and we fly planes and we stay in hotels and we like comedy and we like music, that we're alive, that being a Christian isn't the end of your life, it's the beginning. It's exciting to me.[122]

That week, T. D. spoke to more than forty thousand men in the Georgia Dome in an event that was broadcast live around the world in English and Spanish. In South Africa, men at Drakenstein Prison, where former President Nelson Mandela once was imprisoned, got up at two o'clock in the morning to watch the event. NAACP President Kweisi Mfume sat on the stage and former baseball player and recovering drug addict Darryl Strawberry was among those in the audience.

If MegaFest was a hit among attendees, it was viewed skeptically by critics, both religious and secular. The religious critics decried the lack of religious credentials of some of the speakers and entertainment acts. For instance, Suze Orman was well-known around the country for her financial acumen, but her spiritual testimony was unknown by the public. Steve Harvey was a very funny comedian but was also known to use questionable language in his comedy act. Magic Johnson was one of the most infamous HIV-positive individuals in the world.

In 2005, Jakes explained that he was careful when inviting secular artists, but that there was also a higher reason behind his methods. "We've tried to carefully and selectively choose people who are working in a secular environment but had a Christian walk, especially for people that we are trying to draw back into the Christian fold."[123]

Jakes understands that the testimony of forgiven people gives hope to others seeking forgiveness—hope that they will not be judged forever by the mistakes they have made in the past. Jakes said that when Steve Harvey was invited to appear, the comedian was moved to tears.

He was so excited and so touched that he, by his accord, called and said he wanted to do it again. He's also started to attend our church more regularly. You have to build a bridge. The Bible says, *"He that winneth souls is wise."* I think sometimes we are so rigid whom we're willing to talk to and reach out to that we inadvertently close the door to a unique group of people that need to see themselves and see how they fit in our world."[124]

Steve Harvey was so impacted by his appearance at MegaFest that he changed the tone of his comedy act and featured some of the material he used at the conference on his next comedy album.

All told, MegaFest 2004 drew 140,000 people to Atlanta and reached 314 million homes in 235 countries worldwide. In planning MegaFest 2005, Jakes acknowledged the impact they had made in their first year. "I think we struck a nerve last year. We walked away from it understanding that Christians from everywhere appreciated an opportunity to come together with their family in an environment with ministry that was age and gender appropriate to each member of the family."[125]

The first conference allowed Jakes and his team to work out all of the logistical issues of conducting such a huge event. This is not to say that hosting it a second time would be easy for them, but at least it was a path they had already trodden. T. D. knew what he was trying to bring about with MegaFest and felt that there was more to be accomplished by the event. "I think the things that I deal with are the things that everybody confronts with whether you are black, white, red, brown, rich or poor. You struggle with life, you struggle with your own fears, age, crises, children, abuse, traumas. It's a 'you can do it' message. It's a positive message."[126]

MegaFest 2005 director Derek Williams expressed his desire for the conference to have a positive impact on families.

> Family is very important, and that's something that Bishop Jakes has been talking about for many years. For America and the world, this is an event that allows men, mothers, children to all do their own activities separately, but when they come back as a unit, there's much more there.[127]

The festivities at MegaFest 2005 followed much of the same format as the first year. It included shows hosted by Tom Joyner and J. Anthony Brown, as well as Steve Harvey and Rickey Smiley. There were concerts featuring Kirk Franklin and Mary Mary. There was also a "Women of Purpose" concert that honored Coretta Scott King, featuring pop legend Gladys Knight, as well as Stephanie Wells and Vickie Winans. During the concert, Knight sang her popular hit from the 1970s, "Midnight Train to Georgia," in honor of Mrs. King. Again, critics bemoaned the fact that Ms. Knight was a Mormon and said she had no place at the conference. Williams defended her appearance, saying, "The purpose of the 'Woman of Purpose' concert was to honor Coretta Scott King. Gladys Knight and the others were there for that reason. We wouldn't put (Knight) on the platform to preach."[128]

> Jakes understands that the testimony of forgiven people gives hope to others seeking forgiveness.

There were a number of Christian speakers at the conference, several of them women. Paula White, former co-pastor of Without Walls International Church, spoke of how she considered T. D. and Serita Jakes to be her spiritual parents and how they had mentored her in so many ways. Juanita Bynum encouraged the crowd to believe and walk in faith no matter what circumstances they faced in life. Bishop Paul Morton from New Orleans spoke to the crowd of mostly African-Americans, telling them, "I think I see positive things happening, but we're still complaining about what happened four hundred years ago. Pastors are here from every denomination trying to reach the African-American community and bring them to the next level."[129]

Even though the attendees were largely African-American, there were people there of all races. Darlene Bishop was a keynote speaker and spoke of bringing the races together. "This has shown America that when God's people get together, we can make a difference for Christ. It's not like 'I'm white and they're black.' We are all one people. Jesus is our common denominator."[130]

Among the other speakers were Reverend Jamal-Harrison Bryant, pastor of Baltimore's Empowerment Temple, the fastest growing African Methodist Episcopal (AME) church on record; Bishop Noel Jones, pastor of City of Refuge in south central Los Angeles, a congregation of more than ten thousand; Bishop Eddie Long, pastor of New Birth Missionary Baptist Church outside Atlanta, a congregation of over twenty-five thousand; and Marcos Witt, Hispanic pastor of Lakewood Church in Houston, the largest church in America with a weekly attendance in excess of forty thousand.

MegaFest 2005 also addressed family prosperity. Financial guru Suze Orman returned and gave an address entitled, "Young, Fabulous, and Broke." She provided advice about ways to raise a credit rating and the reasons to buy a home. Known for financial advice, Orman did offer some spiritual as well. "I think [God] blesses you whether you believe in Him or not, but, if you don't understand the power of God within yourself, you will never have what you should have, and even if you have it, you're not going to keep it."[131]

Many families began to use MegaFest as an excuse for a family reunion. Some simply treated the event as their annual vacations. Those who were not particularly religious could enjoy the music and comedy acts, but would be exposed to a positive message as well.

Once again, the event had corporate sponsors, such as Coca-Cola, Bank of America, and American Airlines, as Jakes continued his effort to introduce corporate America to the Christian market. Jakes also wanted to position black consumers as more than simply gangbangers and rap stars, but people with high values who will do business with corporations that respect those values.

The 2005 event was not as well attended as the previous year, with just over 100,000 in attendance compared with 140,000 in 2004, but it still made a significant economic impact on Atlanta, bringing about $125 million into the city. MegaFest was still one of the largest and most lucrative events hosted by the city.

CRITICISM BY THE BLACK PRESS

Some within the black community began to criticize MegaFest in 2005, specifically those of the local black press who complained that African-Americans were not getting their share of the money spent in Atlanta to create the event. Earlier that summer, Jakes had addressed the National Newspaper Publishers Association, a federation of more than two hundred black newspapers, and pledged to partner with them. At the meeting Jakes said, "Today is the beginning of a reconciliation between the black church and the black press. I see our union as an opportunity to extend our voice to your audience and extend your voice to our audience."[132]

After that meeting, the black press fully expected to receive a major amount of the advertising revenue for MegaFest 2005. Yet this was not the case. The *Atlanta Voice* printed a story, subsequently reprinted in black newspapers across the country, in which John Smith Sr., president of the National Association of Black Journalist and publisher of the *Atlanta Inquirer*, complained that not one dime was spent by MegaFest 2005 with Atlanta's black press. The *Atlanta Voice*, and a syndication of black newspapers, subsequently printed an article that presented charges and countercharges regarding the controversy. In the story, Jakes responded angrily, "To be called cheap in that article was an insult. It also upset me that rather than come to me directly for resolution, this matter was discussed publicly in the press." Jakes continued, "Every time I don't spend money now I am a bad guy. You don't resolve a business conflict with 'yellow' journalism."

The local black press did not appreciate being accused of "yellow" journalism. *Atlanta Voice* editor Stan Washington responded by saying, "It's only 'yellow' journalism if it is untrue or if it is a deliberate attempt to smear someone. The story was neither. It was truth. No one is out to slander Jakes or his organization." Smith also voiced his response: "The story was not unfair. In my conversation with [Jakes], he said the story was one-sided, but we did not know how to get to him." [133]

> Some within the local black press complained that African-Americans were not getting their share of the money spent in Atlanta to create MegaFest.

The complaints were strong and unending. "We got nothing; he's not spending anything with Atlanta's black newspapers," said Cheryl Mainor, advertising and marketing director for the *Atlanta Voice*.[134]

Advertising dollars, it seemed, had been spent with black-owned and -oriented radio stations while black newspapers were offered only free tickets to the event in exchange for advertising space. Jakes and the MegaFest management describe the situation not as a snub but as a simple business decision. As Jakes later explained,

> I am not opposed to marketing in the Black press, but the article makes it sound like I put money into other print media and that I deliberately snubbed the Black press….With the exception of ads we ran in the papers of our MegaFest media sponsors and the ad we ran in the *Atlanta Journal-Constitution* thanking the city for their hospitality…we did not buy ads in any newspaper, including the Black press.[135]

Jakes further explained the purpose of his summer appearance before the NNPA.

They invited me to the Black press [convention] and we did say that we were going to work together....They did not say that the cost of admission was how much money I spent....If that was what the meeting was about....They need to send a business proposal to a marketing director. And it can't be done in June for a [MegaFest] meeting that occurs in August because we bought our ads months and months ago, and we do it nationally and not locally.[136]

Atlanta Voice advertising and marketing director Cheryl Mainor disputed that account.

The sales department began talking to Cheryl Thomas with The Potter's House in January. In May, they committed to running an ad before MegaFest. In July, Jacquelyn Jakes called and said they had exhausted their local advertising budget and would we like to barter for tickets to their entertainment events.[137]

Jakes and NNPA have tried to make peace and Jakes now says, "I've discussed this with NNPA president John Smith, and I've concluded that the whole matter is largely a misunderstanding."[138]

THE CONFERENCES CONTINUE

Conferences have continued to be a major vehicle for T. D. Jakes to communicate his message, reach out to unchurched men and women, and raise his own public profile.

In the spring of 2006, Jakes hosted a retreat for men at the Gaylord Texan in Grapevine, Texas, called For Men Only. The purpose of the event was to provide men an opportunity "to participate in informal meetings and seminars focused on faith, family, and business."[139] In addition to Jakes, the retreat featured Bishop Eddie Long, Dr. Charles Abams, Dr. Myles Munroe, and entertainer Fred Hammond. Every effort was made to maintain a male-oriented focus for the three thousand men who attended. Instead of flowers or frills up front, the stage was completely bare except for two large motorcycles on each side. Vendors offered menswear, complimentary haircuts, and male hygiene products, as well as a collection of huge SUVs. A basketball court was set up on the side for pickup games.

In the summer of 2006, MegaFest was held for the third time. Tickets for the event were thirty-five dollars, giving one access to all the concerts, messages, and other venues. MegaFest 2006 included many of the speakers and performers who had been a part of the earlier events as well as an *American Idol*-type competition showcasing up-and-coming gospel stars. For kids, there was a science show featuring laser lights and "flights" in a hovercraft-like vehicle that made them feel as though they were in space.

> Ramset shared that the biggest reason people don't have more money is the person looking back at them in the mirror each morning.

One new attraction was Christian financial guru and author Dave Ramsey, who addressed an enthusiastic crowd. Ramsey teaches stewardship in a way that few others can. He comes across like a motivating sports coach, mixing humor with sound financial advice. He explained that there are eight hundred Bible verses on the subject of money and shared that the biggest reason people don't have more money is the person looking back at them in the mirror each morning.

Although the focus of the conference continued to be the family, it became a special event because it marked T. D. Jakes's thirtieth anniversary in ministry. An anniversary celebration was held at the Georgia Dome, and the attendees were treated to five hours of gospel music with a twist of soul; the celebration featured such artists as Aretha Franklin,

Donnie McClurkin, Shirley Caesar, Kirk Franklin, Kelly Price, Fred Hammond, Vanessa Bell Armstrong, and Jeff Majors, as well as The Potter's House Mass Choir. Many celebrities attended to contribute their words of honor and appreciation for T. D. Among those who addressed the crowd were Emmitt Smith, Michael Irvin, Will Smith, Boris Kudjoe, LL Cool J, Star Jones, and Tom Joyner. T. D.'s children also spoke and congratulated their father on his many years of ministry. Touched by this, Jakes later remarked, "If somebody else says you are wonderful and the people you live with don't, then you have failed. It is far more important that the people who know you the best think well of you because they get to see every part of you."[140]

At the end of the night, the crowd was informed that portions of the proceeds for the night would go to benefit the survivors of Hurricane Katrina and the construction of wells in Africa.

Reflecting on his years in ministry, Jakes said,

It's been an amazing journey and culminating on the thirtieth celebration gives me a moment to reflect on so many experiences that happened along the way—the very meager beginnings and how God blessed me in so many ways. It's a moment to reflect and appreciate all of the things that He has done.[141]

Immediately afterward, TDJ Enterprises conducted a conference in Jacksonville, Florida, called BEST (Black Economic Success Training). It was designed to be both motivational and educational, equipping people to reach, maintain, and build upon greater levels of success than they ever thought possible. Alvin Brown, chairman of the National Black MBA Association, was among the many speakers. He encouraged young people to pursue higher education as a route to develop their leadership potential.

The last year that MegaFest was held was 2006. The management of the conference reported that even with all of the ticket and merchandise sales, the conference lost about ten million dollars each year. In 2006, Jakes had to fly twelve hundred volunteers from Dallas to Atlanta, where he provided housing and a per diem for them. In addition to the criticism of the Atlanta black press, the city of Dallas publicly questioned Jakes regarding why a major conference hosted by a Dallas church, and creating huge amounts of revenue, was being held in Georgia.

When the announcement was made that there would be no Mega-Fest 2007, it was said there were plans to have a MegaFest 2008. But in the summer of 2007, it was announced that the plans for MegaFest 2008 had been cancelled. Jakes released a statement that said, "At this point and time, we have decided to focus our efforts on our other events, such as For Ladies Only, For Men Only, the Pastors and Leadership Conference, and our Faith for Africa missionary efforts, to name a few."[142]

In January 2008, however, the ministry released plans for arguably the biggest and most ambitious MegaFest ever, announcing that in October 2008, the conference would go international by moving from Atlanta to Johannesburg, South Africa. As part of the ministry's press release, Jakes stated,

> At the previous MegaFest events, we had people attend from all over the world, all ethnicities, all religions; so many different cultures were in the room. As I looked out, the feel was so much more aligned to an international event than a U.S.-specific event. I believe the true purpose of the ministry is to go beyond your traditional walls and minister to the world. MegaFest International provides us with that platform.

AFRICA: THE ROLE OF JOSEPH

We didn't come here with medicine
and doctors and businessmen and musicians
to simply entertain you—we came to empower you.

—T. D. Jakes

Chapter Ten

AFRICA: THE ROLE OF JOSEPH

T. D. Jakes started going to Africa in 1995, about the time his ministry moved to the Dallas area. Since then, he has made several trips to the nations of Kenya, Uganda, South Africa, the Ivory Coast, and Nigeria. He describes his travels to Africa in this way:

> Even though I've traveled to many countries in Africa and experienced the uniqueness of each one, from the bush of Ghana to the resorts of Cape Town to the Nigerian Palace where I dined with President Obosanjo, I find one constant. My abiding respect and awe for the continent and its varied beauties only grows richer and deeper."[143]

Jakes has often referred to his first trip to Africa as unbelievably moving and fulfilling.

> As I sat on the aircraft preparing myself to disembark, I entered into the final landing stages of my flight on South African Air. My thoughts were filled with expectations of what the trip would bring. However, none of my premonitions would have prepared me for the impact that this trip would have on my life. In retrospect, I realize that I was walking closer and closer to a reflected image of my own culture and people. I thought I would see the African people as a significant, but different people than myself.[144]

Africa: The Role of Joseph

During a sermon, he shared what it was like for him, an African-American, to return to Africa.

> It is like a set of twins, separated at birth, one raised in one part of the world and the other one raised in another part of the world. Then years later they come together for the first time. They look at each other for the first time. They say to each other, "Wow, you look so familiar. You look so familiar to me! I swear I know you from somewhere. I just can't remember where. Your food smells like mine. When you dance, you move your body like mine. When you clap your hands you clap your hands like I clap my hands! It is good for us to be together, again; to sit together, again; to worship together, again."[145]

HIS LIFE'S MISSION

Over the years, Jakes has made quite an impact on the various African nations he has visited, just as they have made an impact on him. On each of his visits, he has been greeted as one would greet a world leader. The African press makes a huge media event of his appearances. They remark about his travel by private jet and the style of his clothing. When Serita travels with him, they mention her attire as well.

T. D.'s grandmother had told him about family members who had been slaves. In 2006, Jakes allowed his DNA to be analyzed for the PBS television program *African-American Lives*. His Y chromosome determined that he was descended from the Igbo people of what is now Nigeria. On the program he stated,

> It's kind of weird because for the last ten years I've been increasingly focused on Africa, doing ministerial and philanthropic work there, including in Nigeria. I went to Logos, and I had the most odd feeling of being home. I thought, "You look so familiar to me: your humor, your music, your food. I swear I know you

from somewhere but I don't know where."....My Nigerian friends are all going to say, "See, I told you."[146]

Even before the test made it conclusive, Jakes saw it as his responsibility to assist those he viewed as his forefathers. He recently spoke about this powerful vision:

While I was in the Ivory Coast of Africa, I went through the gate of no return where the slaves left and they said they wouldn't be back. And I walked through that gate as a sign that we did return and we are okay. My heart's desire is to lead thousands and thousands of African-Americans back through that gate in my lifetime....Not even to lead, but just be a part of a pilgrimage to break the curse that they said we would not come back. That is so burning in me I get emotional every time I think about it. I can hardly talk about it without being moved to tears. It would fulfill my life's mission."[147]

He speaks and writes about his strong emotional attachment to Africa and of how much he enjoys meeting people who so purely represent his own ancestry and the culture of his heritage. Jakes's desire, however, goes far beyond merely meeting them. He deeply wants to make a difference in their lives.

My goal as I travel back and forth to Africa is not just to preach, but to bring together teams of doctors to come with medicine. I just love the people. I love their cultures. I love their diverse foods, and I feel needed there. I think there is a way that we, particularly as African-Americans, can respond in a unique and fresh way to the plight of Africa. As much as the Caucasian missionaries have done in the African countries through the centuries, they cannot do the work that African-Americans can do. I do not think they can replace the role of Joseph, and I use Joseph to speak of an African-American who was sold into slavery but has a responsibility to connect with his brothers again. As for me, it was a family reunion of sorts to be reconnected with my ancestral roots, and to be needed to bring wells and water and food and medicine blessed me with this feeling."[148]

Jakes went to the White House to meet with President George W. Bush on Africa and to push for increased aid. He later reinforced his feelings in a letter so there would be no doubt about the depth of his feelings. He reminded the president that Africa is to African-Americans what Israel is to Jewish-Americans.

Because of his love for the people of the African continent, he has made every effort to stretch his impact there to share the gospel of Jesus Christ. His television program began broadcasting to South Africa in 1999, and the program is now broadcast to other African countries as well. Soweto, South Africa, was the site of his first international crusade. Leaders of the African nations began to take notice of the growing influence Jakes was having and invited him to speak at the coronation ceremonies of Ghana tribal king Kingsley Fletcher in 1999.

> Jakes reminded President Bush that Africa is to African-Americans what Israel is to Jewish-Americans.

When Jakes visits Africa, his message doesn't change. He is a strong messenger for Jesus Christ, but he also preaches about upward mobility for black people, just as in the United States. In January 2005, Jakes was the guest of honor at a dinner in Kenya where two thousand people paid twenty-five dollars each to listen to him speak on business success. During his talk, he drew on examples from the Bible. Jakes said,

> Preachers have to go beyond merely preaching and start empowering people economically. It is the role of Christian leaders to

win souls for Christ, but it is also our duty to raise the standards of living of the people. Poverty is one of the most dangerous slave masters on earth today. As church leaders, we must never sit back and watch our people continue to be under its shackles.[149]

The Kenyan dinner had been organized by the first lady of Kenya, Beat Bisangwa. Her excitement at hosting the meeting, as well as emceeing the evening, was evident when she said to the African press, "I cannot believe I am sitting in the same room with Bishop T. D. Jakes."[150] Also in attendance was Apolo Nsibambi, prime minister of Uganda, and Luke Orombi, the Archbishop of Uganda.

The wife of Uganda's president, Janet Museveni, who was at the dinner as well, spoke of her appreciation and admiration for Bishop Jakes. Many other African dignitaries were present also, including a number of members of the Ugandan parliament. In Africa, T. D. Jakes seems to be viewed as something more than a pastor. Again, he is treated in a way similar to that of leaders of nations and seems to have a great deal of influence over many people.

SEEING THE NEED

Jakes was deeply touched by the need in Africa on his very first trip to Nigeria. He was walking down the street with a number of African pastors when children began to group around him, perhaps attracted by his colorful clothing. As he looked around, he was moved by their obvious poverty and began to reach into his pockets for all of the loose money he could find. As he began to pass the money out to the children swarming around him, he noticed two things. First, his African host pastors were amused by what he was doing, chuckling as he tried to meet the need of every child he could. Second, he quickly noticed how the children gathering around him multiplied. It seemed that every time he gave to one child, two more appeared in his or her place.

Africa: The Role of Joseph

Afraid that he had committed some kind of cultural faux pas, he asked his hosts why they were laughing. They let him know that what he was doing was not a bad thing, but that no one person could possibly meet the needs of all the children of Nigeria. They were multiplying faster than the world's resources could be gathered.

Jakes also observed that one of the greatest health crises in the world today is the HIV/AIDS crisis in Africa, the most infected continent on earth. He teamed with former United Nations ambassador and former mayor of Atlanta Andrew Young to open the world's eyes to begin to see the seriousness of this issue. Together they issued a statement:

> We are American Christians of African descent. We have seen the fight for apartheid. We participated in Live Aid concerts and hummed the melody of "We Are the World." We have witnessed plane after plane, ship after ship carrying manna from heaven—abundant amounts of food for the people of Africa. Together, we share a commitment with millions of missionaries and active socially minded groups around the world to feed the hungry, heal the sick, and to set at liberty those who are oppressed. So why are there still so many admonitions to keep caring for Africa?
>
> Recently, we were invited, along with 20 colleagues, to meet with Secretary of State Condoleezza Rice in an effort to continue an established bipartisan tradition of church-state cooperation in areas of need and opportunity. President Bush's recent signing of the African Growth and Opportunity Act extension is but one example of his appreciation of Africa's importance to the U.S. as a trading partner and supplier of strategic minerals. But is it enough?
>
> In a word, no. Africa is crying out for more than a place in the international buffet line. UNAIDS (the United Nations program on HIV/AIDS) has published a haunting report that concludes more than eighty million living in Africa could perish

from AIDS by 2025. Unless concerted actions are taken, another catastrophe awaits.[151]

The remainder of the statement urged the G-8 economic leaders to help relieve African nations of the insurmountable debt they had amassed. If they were forced to pay back their debt to the nations and financial institutions of the world, their citizens would never receive the food and medical care they desperately needed. There also would simply not be enough funds left to rebuild the infrastructures required to develop their economies.

T. D. Jakes remains committed to making a difference on the African continent in as many countries as he can. In his original statement, he explained the steps he was taking to do this.

> I have put together a task force to explore ways that we, as African-American churches, can become givers and empower our disjointed family with help spiritually, economically, and academically. I am asking the Christian church of all colors to break the silence both here and there and acknowledge all racism as a sin, repent of it, and challenge all others to do the same. I would like to go back to South Africa with a scholarship fund, a plan for economic empowerment, and the reconciliation of African-Americans to Africans. The reconciliation of the Christian church to its original Pauline mandate is that there be no division between Greek nor Jew (racism), bond nor free (socialism), male nor female (genders).[152]

Jakes's ambitions for Africa are not small, but he is determined to make a difference. On a trip to Nigeria, he did not miss a chance to encourage the people there to make the most of their opportunities economically, both personally and nationally.

> All countries have great challenges, and Nigeria is not far removed from those issues as well. It's very important that we see

economic empowerment down to all people and all citizens of Nigeria so that they will have the opportunity to achieve their dreams. Certainly, we will love to see Nigeria reach its goals and be prepared to maintain all of its citizens, able to better their lifestyles both economically and morally. I really know that Nigeria will achieve that because conversations between Nigerians and African-Americans are geared towards strengthening one another. We share what we have learned from history, and it will really help to expedite the process.[153]

THE SOURCE OF LIFE: WATER

The focus of the work of The Potter's House in Africa has been the nation of Kenya. When T. D. first went there, he brought money for medicine and delivered seven tons of food to regions ravaged by drought. While there, however, he learned that the people of Kenya could go a long way toward caring for their own needs if they had sources of clean and plentiful water.

Clean water is crucial to tackling the health problems of the Third World. So many easily treatable illnesses are killing men, women, and children each day due to their drinking, cooking, and bathing with contaminated water. One Kenyan woman described life in the bush this way: "We don't normally wash our children because we say don't let the child get used to water because we don't have water so we never wash our babies."[154]

Many African children are taken out of school when they get old enough to carry water a great distance because their parents are busy working to scrape out the barest of existences for their families. If clean water were available nearby, the children would be able to continue their educations and better their lives.

> Clean water is crucial to tackling the health problems of the Third World.

Clean water would improve the health of livestock, which, in turn, would improve the health of the people because of better meat, milk, eggs, and other animal products. Clean water would help the people to raise better crops. In addition, limited access to clean water has become a source of conflict between various tribes and other groups of people, a problem that would be alleviated if all had equal access to it.

There is, however, an engineering challenge to drilling wells in Kenya. To dig a well in America, it is necessary to drill an average of eighty feet. In Kenya, due to years of drought conditions and sandy soil, it is often necessary to drill an average of seven hundred feet or more in order to reach water reserves.

> Due to years of drought conditions and sandy soil, it is often necessary to drill an average of seven hundred feet or more in order to reach water reserves.

In response to this growing problem and to what he had learned about the need for clean water, Jakes began raising money to drill wells in Kenya. He often used his pulpit, speaking engagements, and media interviews to communicate the need for clean water wells.

African-Americans have reached the point that they can go back and help brothers and sisters. Water is the source of life, and for thousands of families living in Kenya, and in much of rural Africa, that life source is held hostage by plague and pestilence as they are forced to bathe in and drink what amounts to liquid disease. Our focus is to ensure that in order to quench their thirst and feed their children, parents are no longer pressed into these unimaginable circumstances.[155]

In January 2005, T. D. worked closely with the Kenyan parliament and broke ground on three boreholes to be drilled in different parts of the Rift Valley province. They also drilled a well in an almost barren region called Enkaroni, a Maasai word meaning "the place of no water." Since this well was installed, water has flowed freely into a small reservoir and into two troughs for thousands of families to use for drinking, cooking, and bathing, free from worry or fear of illness from using contaminated water.

To date, The Potter's House has provided the resources to dig thirteen wells in the extremely dry, rural terrain. In a place where drilling came up dry, a ten-mile pipeline was laid, delivering water to some twenty thousand people, over a million goats and sheep, and nearly half a million head of cattle. A local Dallas TV news reporter accompanied the team and interviewed Ronnie Guynes, who helped oversee the mission. "We've dug here for boreholes and we've tried to hit water and we've hit dry holes. There's a drought here in Africa, in Kenya, and many Maasi have died. Their cattle have died and they need water desperately, and we're pushing to make this happen as soon as we can."[156]

Jakes has spread the word to the Kenyans about what The Potter's House and others are doing, and has even used the opportunity to illustrate the love of God and the love people should have for one another.

> The money for the drilling of these wells comes from people across the sea. These people have never met you; they don't know what you look like. Yet, they love you enough to pay money so you can have water. If people who don't know you love you so much, why is it that you—who live next door to each other—cannot love each other?[157]

EDUCATION AND MEDICINE

In addition to digging wells, The Potter's House has raised money to impact education and medical treatment. If Kenya is going to make the strides necessary to be competitive in the twenty-first century, the young people there need a modern education. Today, twenty-two hundred students who attend the Kawangware Primary School in Kenya now have a window to the world through a computer lab by The Potter's House. Jakes commented on the lab, "Technology is spanning the globe, and these children in Nairobi should have all the access to doors of opportunity that any other child does around the world. These computers will now provide them the keys to open these doors."[158] In October 2006, the lab was dedicated to the memory of T. D.'s late mother, Odith Jakes. Because of Odith's influence as an educator and mentor for many young people during her life, it seemed appropriate to name this project, which would help so many young people, after her.

> If Kenya is going to make the strides necessary to be competitive in the twenty-first century, the young people there need a modern education.

In 2005, more than six thousand Kenyans received medical care because The Potter's House sent organized teams of doctors and nurses to serve in the nation's medical camps. Pharmaceuticals valued at more than two hundred thousand dollars, as well as seven thousand pairs of eyeglasses, were distributed in several districts of Kenya. Melchizedek Hospital, located in a slum area called Kawangware, was able to complete a new wing—the T. D. Jakes Wing—housing a maternity ward, intensive care units, and an operating room.

Jakes led a group of over three hundred people to Kenya, including a skilled team of one hundred and twenty medical professionals and a one hundred and forty voice choir to record an original album. They brought hundreds of thousands of dollars in medical supplies, plans to dig more wells, food, and hopes of stirring up new business opportunities for Kenyans. Once again, members of the Dallas media accompanied the group on its trip, which lasted from September 26 to October 2, 2005. T. D. proclaimed, "African-Americans may have left in slave ships, but we're returning in 747s."[159] T. D. wanted as much publicity for the trip to Kenya as possible in order to create greater awareness among the American public about the desperate situation there. It was considered to be the largest group of slave descendents ever to visit Africa as U.S. missionaries.

During the trip, a delegation of mission partners visited the Suswa and Mai-Mahiu areas to commission three wells. That year, "more than one hundred and twenty people had been killed in conflicts stemming from a rival tribe's blocking of a stream that watered Maasai livestock."[160] Members of Church World Service (CWS) and The Potter's House mobilized elders from both tribes to work on a water-sharing solution. According to Moses Ole Sakuda, a CWS associate director, the project was received "with joy and praise" and "brought peace to the region."[161]

The delegation later visited three impoverished areas where it handed out food and medicine. Local residents began to line up as early as six o'clock in the morning to see the medical personnel. The joint team of American and Kenyan doctors and nurses examined patients, performed X-rays, and conducted laboratory tests as needed.

The delegation traveled to the Kajiado district, an area about a two-hour drive from Nairobi. There they dedicated a well and visited the two-day medical camp that had been set up. Some of the people in that area had not seen a doctor for more than thirty years. Bishop Jakes led a prayer meeting at a nearby village where twenty-three people had recently been killed over water disputes.

Those traveling with Jakes's team, although primarily African-Americans, were mostly middle-class, middle-aged people who were experiencing something completely new. On this part-vacation, part-missions trip, they saw nations with modern skyscrapers and highways but without commonly accepted amenities. T. D.'s goal was to share an African culture and experience with this large group of people—both the good and the unusual.

At one of the villages they visited, a play was performed in their honor in which boys portrayed village elders who mediated a disagreement. In the play, the agreed-upon solution was for a young girl from the village to marry an older man. She wept because she did not want to marry this man. He was too old and this was not how she had envisioned her life. In the end, however, she married the man, the disagreement was resolved, and everyone lived happily ever after—except for her. The local community celebrated the play. Some in Jakes's group asked their hosts how old girls of their village are when they get married. The answer was fifteen or sixteen. The Americans shook their heads in disbelief. In Africa, this was the norm; in America, this was completely unacceptable. T. D. Jakes, a man who in many ways developed his ministry by reaching out to abused and disenfranchised women, had to smile politely as women were portrayed doing something he had fought his entire life to free women from.

The following Sunday afternoon there was an outdoor service, which had been planned for some time. Local pastors who organized the event predicted that as many as three hundred fifty thousand people might attend—not only from Kenya but neighboring countries as well. When the day of the event came, they were proven wrong. Nearly a million people amassed for the outdoor service—as many people as when Pope John Paul II had visited Kenya. On the vast hillside amphitheater sat Kenyans, Ugandans, Sudanese, and Nigerians, to name just a few. The people of Africa had come together to worship God and to hear from this man of God from America.

Looking out over the crowd was like looking out at an ocean of people. Some wore white shirts and ties that could be deemed western "church clothes." Others, particularly the women, wore colorful, flowing, traditional robes. Many carried white handkerchiefs, which they waved in the air whenever Jakes said something that excited them. On the stage, behind the pulpit, were beautiful banners of white, red, and green. The stage was about fifty feet wide and had covered areas on each side for singers and musicians, as well as for special guests. The stage was in a park in front of a large lake, with the city of Nairobi rising up in the background.

Bishop Jakes preached two messages of hope and expectancy. He used the life of the patriarch Joseph to describe the situation between African-Americans and Africans. Joseph was taken away from his family into slavery. Years later, however, he would be the source of survival for his people. The events in his life that had seemed so bad had been used by God for good. Jakes told the crowd that the brothers and sisters lost to slavery would provide the resources that Africa needs to renew itself and survive, becoming better and stronger than ever before. He encouraged them to believe God for greater things. He spoke not of American prosperity with cars and brick homes, but of seeing children grow up and receive educations that would better their lives.

> Jakes described poverty as the slave master of the 21st century. Going unchecked, it steals the will of whomever it captures.

He described poverty as the slave master of the twenty-first century. Going unchecked, it steals the will of whomever it captures. He encouraged the crowd to make certain that every Kenyan had something to eat, somewhere to stay, and something to wear "because you can't be free until your brothers are free!"[162] He reminded them to focus on freeing the children because they represented the future. He envisioned Africans living together in peace where violence, anger, and hatred are not the norm. He told them that God would take the anointing that was on his life and share it with the people of Africa to do miracles in their lives.

Another missionary outreach trip to Kenya took place in 2006 and included eighteen people who went to perform more work in the name of the Lord. Although far fewer in number than those from the year before, they still made an impact. They ran a two-day medical camp where approximately fifteen hundred people were treated. The people were treated by Kenyan doctors, who were paid by the ministry in an attempt to help the local economy.

The Potter's House had collected about fifteen hundred pairs of shoes, which were distributed to many people who had never owned a pair. Two hundred thousand dollars' worth of medical supplies were also distributed, as well as five thousand bottles of vitamins, school supplies, soap, and other items.

Bringing the Message Home

Bishop Jakes has been at the forefront of encouraging the United States, as well as other Western countries, to assist African countries in overcoming the obstacles to their economic development. Besides being a prominent voice encouraging the forgiveness of Third World debt, Jakes has encouraged more help for the millions of Africans suffering from HIV and AIDS.

Jakes has publicly applauded President George W. Bush for providing three times more aid to countries in Africa than any other president before him, but he was also a cosigner of a letter from a group of African-American clergymen to the White House encouraging the president to accept a challenge from then British Prime Minister Tony Blair to provide twenty-five billion dollars in aid to countries on the African continent. The letter expressed the real possibility that if more was not done to assist the people of Africa, they would become ripe recruits for terrorist groups. The clergymen pointed out that while the cost of war in the Middle East and congressional tax cuts were in the hundreds of billions of dollars, the cost of helping African nations is estimated to be only twenty-five billion dollars.

The ministry to Africa is an ongoing project of The Potter's House and T. D. Jakes. The problems there are immense and did not appear overnight. Thus, they will not likely be solved overnight either. Since T. D. Jakes is a man who has been on the national stage for only about fifteen years, however, and who turned fifty in 2007, his impact on Africa may only have just begun.

CONTROVERSY AND CRITICISM

Controversy goes with the turf....It [the accusations] didn't hurt me at all. It gave me an opportunity to give clarity to what my convictions were to what I believe. And having done that, it seems not to be an issue to people, and it certainly wasn't an issue to me.

—T. D. Jakes[163]

The concept of the Godhead is a mystery that has baffled Christians for years. With our limited minds we try to comprehend a limitless God. How can we explain one God but three distinct manifestations?

—T. D. Jakes[164]

Chapter Eleven

CONTROVERSY AND CRITICISM

Criticism and controversy have followed T. D. Jakes just as congregations, fame, and financial blessing have. Perhaps all those things naturally go hand in hand. In truth, however, controversy in the life and ministry of T. D. Jakes likely started in the obscurity and anonymity of the West Virginia mountains when he began to slip away from the Baptist church of his youth to visit a local Pentecostal church. At the time, Jakes was likely not aware of all the differences in theology and doctrine between the two bodies. All Tommy Jakes knew was that the Pentecostal service was a lot more fun and exciting than the Baptist service. Certainly, the Baptist service was not as liturgical as in a formal Methodist or Episcopal church, but the Pentecostal service was more lively and appealing to the young man. Over time, Jakes accepted the Pentecostal style as his own, not understanding the controversy that the peculiar doctrine of that church would create later in his life and ministry. Beyond the upbeat music, shouting, and hand waving, this particular branch of the Pentecostal church held on to a doctrine known as "Oneness."

PENTECOSTAL ROOTS

The Pentecostal church began in the late nineteenth century when the Methodist denomination began to evolve into more of a mainline church that the one John and Charles Wesley had founded, which was radical in its outreach and approach to holiness. It shifted from a focus on the moving of the Holy Spirit in the life of the believer to a focus on the intellect. In the eyes of many, this was seen as a move toward a more theologically liberal belief and practice.

This shift did not sit well with some, and they began to leave the Methodist Church to create other churches and denominations. Among these newer churches and denominations were the Nazarene Church, the Pentecostal Holiness Church, and the Free Methodist Church.

At the beginning of the twentieth century, another movement branched off from the Methodist holiness tradition. It started in Kansas, soon spread to Texas, and finally emerged in Los Angeles, California. This offshoot was what would become the Pentecostal movement and, in the second half of the twentieth century, the charismatic movement.

> Unaware of the differences in theology and doctrine between the two, all Tommy Jakes knew was that the Pentecostal service was a lot more fun and exciting than the Baptist service.

William Seymour, an African-American man who was blind in one eye, had been filled with the Holy Spirit and spoken in tongues while attending school in Kansas. The school was run by a white man named Charles Parham, leader of the Apostolic Faith Movement, who taught that Christians ought to receive a baptism of the Holy Spirit and then begin to speak in other tongues. The purpose of speaking in tongues was not for worship but for missionary evangelism. Seymour traveled from Kansas to Houston and conducted some services there, teaching what he had learned. His preaching was not well accepted, but someone there invited him to preach in Los Angeles. Once again, his message was rejected, and when he went to preach on the second Sunday, he found the church doors padlocked.

Two members of the church, however, Richard and Ruth Asberry, invited him to come to their home and continue speaking. Word about the impromptu meeting spread, and people descended on the home from all over the city. Because there were too many people to meet inside, the porch of the house became a stage as the yard filled with people eager to hear Seymour's message. The crowds became so large and pressed so hard to get closer to Seymour that the porch of the house collapsed. Once again, Seymour's service had to be moved. The only place suitable for so many people was a barn that had formerly been an African Methodist Episcopal Church, located at 312 Azusa Street.

Services at the barn began April 14, 1906. The large room was cleaned as much as possible, considering that its former tenants were horses. Within a month, there would be anywhere from three hundred to fifteen hundred people trying to crowd into the services. News about what God was doing in Los Angeles began to spread across the country, as well as to other nations, and people began arriving from all over to attend the services.

Several things stood out about these services besides the speaking in tongues. People of all races attended: African-Americans, Hispanics, Asians, and Caucasians. This was a time when races did not mix. Nearly everywhere that crowds gathered, there was strict segregation. The church on Azusa Street, however, broke that pattern. In addition, in the early twentieth century, church life tended to be dominated by men, but at Azusa Street, women were also active in the services. They were allowed to address the congregation in the same way men did. This was fourteen years before women would be given the right to vote in this country. What would become known as "the Azusa Street revival" was different on many levels, but the primary difference was the manifestation of the Holy Spirit's presence and power through speaking in tongues.

From Los Angeles, the movement began to spread throughout the country like wildfire. Leaders of holiness denominations from all over country would take trains or carriages to get to Los Angeles to attend the services and experience what was happening firsthand. A *Los Angeles Times* reporter tried to define what was going on in a front page story with the headline "Weird Babel of Tongues."

> Breathing strange utterances and mouthing a creed which it would seem no sane mortal could understand, the newest religious sect has started in Los Angeles.[165]

Another local newspaper described the happenings at Azusa Street in this way:

> ...disgraceful intermingling of the races...they cry and make howling noises all day and into the night. They run, jump, shake all over, shout at the top of their voice, spin around in circles, fall out on the sawdust-blanketed floor jerking, kicking, and rolling all over it. Some of them pass out and do not move for hours as though they were dead. These people appear to be mad, mentally deranged, or under a spell. They claim to be filled with the spirit. They have a one eyed, illiterate, Negro as their preacher, who stays on his knees much of the time with his head hidden between the wooden milk crates. He doesn't talk very much but at times he can be heard shouting, "Repent," and he's supposed to be running the thing....They repeatedly sing the same song, "The Comforter Has Come."[166]

Most of the Pentecostal denominations that changed the face of American Christianity in the twentieth century were outgrowths of these meetings.

Charles H. Mason, who had founded the Church of God in Christ, traveled to Los Angeles from Memphis and then returned to Memphis to spread the Pentecostal fire. The Church of God in Christ was primarily a black denomination, but when white pastors who had attended the Azusa Street mission and been filled with the Spirit were later dismissed from their denominations and churches, Mason's church began to ordain the white preachers for ministry as well. In 1916, a group of white ministers organized the Assemblies of God denomination, which is now the largest predominantly white Pentecostal denomination in the world. The Pentecostal Holiness Church also sent representatives to the meetings in Los Angeles, who returned to spread the new movement to their churches as well.

The Azusa Street revival lasted from 1906 to 1909. Various groups across the country then began to carry on Azusa's teachings. Some preachers followed traditional evangelical teachings but added the baptism of the Holy Spirit to their teachings. Others, however, began to teach something different. They taught that Jesus Christ was the only name of God and that people should be baptized only in the name of Jesus, rather than in the name of the Father, the Son, and the Holy Spirit. This teaching, which was soon referred to as "Oneness," used Colossians 2:9 as its defense: *"For in Him dwells all the fullness of the Godhead bodily"* (KJV).

When the Assemblies of God denomination was formed in 1916, it accepted a doctrinal statement that incorporated a more traditional view of the Trinity. When it did this about 20 percent of its ministers—those who had accepted the new Oneness doctrine—left the denomination. Over time, they organized.

T. D. JAKES AND ONENESS

The Pentecostal church that Jakes began attending was part of a small group of churches that were not affiliated with any major denomination and had adopted the Oneness doctrine.

When T. D. founded the Greater Emmanuel Temple of Faith in Montgomery, West Virginia, the church became affiliated with the

Ohio-based Higher Ground Always Abounding Assemblies, a Pentecostal organization with about two hundred affiliated churches. The group had been founded by Bishop Sherman Watkins, who was the presiding bishop when T. D. was ordained. In many ways, Watkins was Jakes's mentor in the early days of his ministry. Watkins recognized the talent in this young man and encouraged him whenever he could. He made certain the door was always open for the young preacher to fill the pulpit of other churches for revivals and youth meetings, which allowed Jakes to practice and learn his craft. Jakes was just a young, rural preacher pastoring a church of less than a dozen people. Nobody knew or cared about what he said or who he was affiliated with. As time went by, however, they would.

> Even with the growth of his ministry and a wider reputation, T. D. Jakes was still only a relatively small fish in a tiny, backwoods pond.

Jakes's ministry grew, and he began to host his first conferences to help other pastors and ministry leaders. He created his first radio ministry and accepted more and more invitations to speak at other churches as his reputation spread. His church began to attract the attention of the white community as well. Though still predominantly African-American, Greater Emmanuel was quickly becoming integrated—nearly 40 percent of its parishioners were white. T. D. was selected by the Higher Ground Always Abounding Assemblies to become an assistant bishop, overseeing other churches and encouraging them along the way. Even with the growth of his ministry and a wider reputation, however, T. D. Jakes was still only a relatively small fish in a tiny, backwoods pond.

Yet with the publication of *Woman Thou Art Loosed!* the bright spotlight of the media began to shine on Jakes. At first, it was his prosperous lifestyle that garnered all the attention. As he began to speak on national television, however, the world started to ask questions. Who is this man? Where did he come from? What does he believe?

Eventually, Jakes resigned from the Higher Ground Always Abounding Assemblies and became bishop over what is called the Pater Alliance, an organization of churches and pastors from denominations that vary from Presbyterian to Baptist to Pentecostal.

The Potter's House was founded as a nondenominational church, and it remains so. T. D. regularly works with fellow Pentecostal ministers such as Bishop Paul Morton of the Full Gospel Baptist Church Fellowship and Bishop Eddie Long of New Birth Missionary Baptist Church. As Jakes says, "I see Pentecostalism more as a way of life than a denomination."[167]

Jakes's Oneness roots haunt his ministry in two vital ways. First, to many he is simply guilty by association with others who firmly hold to its views. Second, Jakes suffers because he refuses to repudiate his past friends and mentors and call them heretics, as his critics demand. These are people who nurtured Jakes in his early ministry, recognizing and calling out his spiritual gifts and legitimizing his ministry when no one else would.

Much of the controversy came to a head in 2000 when one of the most well-respected Christian magazines in the country, *Christianity Today,* called his beliefs into question. In an article, it quoted an apologetics journal that criticized what it perceived to be the doctrine of T. D. Jakes. The journal was a quarterly publication from the Christian Research Institute and quoted an interview that Jakes had given with Los Angeles' KKLA-FM host Jim Coleman in August 1998. It also quoted statements from Jakes's own Web site, which said that God exists in three "manifestations," rather than three Persons. The editor of the journal, Elliot Miller, classified this as "classic modalist language." Modalism defines God as only one Person who takes on the different roles of Father, Son, and Holy Spirit. Traditional Trinitarian teaching describes one God existing eternally as three distinct Persons: Father, Son, and Holy Spirit.

For years, T. D. had chosen to ignore the individual critics who wrote him letters or posted negative remarks on Internet blogs, but he could not ignore a publication like *Christianity Today*. He was allowed to respond with an article entitled, "My Views on the Godhead." In the article Jakes described his spiritual journey and the contributions that certain religious groups had made in his life. In speaking of his association with Oneness, he wrote,

> My association with Oneness people does not constitute assimilation into their ranks any more than my association with the homeless in our city makes me one of them.[168]

He went on to say that he did not consider himself a theologian, but in defending his beliefs, he quoted 1 John:

> *For there are three that bear witness in heaven: the Father, the Word, and the Holy Spirit; and these three are one.*   (1 John 5:7)

He described the attributes of the Father, Son, and Holy Spirit and mentioned how difficult it is for any human illustration to aptly and accurately describe God. He then quoted the apostle Paul.

> *Without controversy great is the mystery of godliness.*
> (1 Timothy 3:16)

He concluded by saying that it was his goal to stay above theological controversies.

> As we seek to dissect the divine, articulate the abstract, and defend what I agree are precious truths, I hope we do not miss the greater message taught by the concept of the Trinity. And that is that three—though distinct—are still one![169]

Jakes's response did little to diffuse the controversy. Today, there are numerous Web sites devoted to telling others that T. D. Jakes is a heretic. Even if Jakes were to declare that he had been deceived in the past, avow that he saw the error of his ways, and condemn all his past friends and associates as heretics, it probably still would not be enough for some.

Jakes continues to speak of the Trinity in his sermons today without hesitation. In one particular sermon entitled "Church on Fire," Jakes spoke of the importance and power of the Holy Spirit as a member of the Trinity, and of how the Holy Spirit constantly reveals the Son to us, drawing us closer to the Father.

A 2006 *Texas Monthly* article described T. D.'s preaching as traditional evangelicalism, saying that he regularly hammers home the importance of Jesus' atoning death and resurrection. The article continued by saying that in his preaching, T. D. holds out Christ as the answer, here and hereafter.[170]

OTHER CRITICISMS

Others condemn Jakes for the people he associates with. For example, they don't like Roberts Liardon because he claims to have been transported to heaven. They don't agree with Jakes inviting Jim Bakker to speak just after he was released from prison. Some object to his association with "charismatic celebrities":

> Jakes patronizes and clearly finds himself among the celebrities of the Charismatic camps. A full-color advertisement on the inside cover of the January *Charisma* announced that Jakes would appear at the August "Victory Word Explosion" in Tulsa, Oklahoma with Benny Hinn, Richard Roberts, Rod Parsley, Joyce Meyer and Jerry Savelle. With this roster, it might better be called "Heresy Explosion."[171]

Other Christian leaders take their share of criticism for merely associating with Jakes. Ed Young of Fellowship Church in Grapevine,

Texas, has invited Jakes to speak from his pulpit on more than one occasion and brags that he has many of T. D.'s sermons on CD and listens to them on an ongoing basis. Bill Hybels of Willow Creek Community Church near Chicago also endured disapproval for inviting Jakes to speak.

Finding an unbiased evaluation of T. D. Jakes is difficult. Is the theological controversy really a debate over the Trinity? Perhaps, but it may also be part of the battle within Christian ranks between those of more conservative or fundamentalist Christian backgrounds and those in the Pentecostal and charismatic movements. It must be said that T. D. Jakes does have some controversial roots.

Yet, fair or not, there will simply always be those who are critical of charismatic and Pentecostal pastors who draw large crowds, sell books, preach on television, and wear fancy clothes. The critics will disagree with their doctrines, with the practice of speaking in tongues, and with the claims of financial blessing and spiritual healing. This debate is older than T. D. Jakes and doesn't promise to end anytime soon.

> Jakes speaks of the importance and power of the Holy Spirit as a member of the Trinity, and of how the Holy Spirit constantly reveals the Son to us, drawing us closer to the Father.

To reject all charismatic and Pentecostal Christians is to reject the fastest-growing portion of the evangelical community in the world. From its humble beginnings on Azusa Street in Los Angeles, the Pentecostal movement has grown to include hundreds of millions of believers all over the world. According to a Pew Forum poll cited in *USA Today*, people who accept Pentecostal beliefs now make up 23 percent of Christians in the United States and one-fourth of the Christians around the world.[172] Charismatic and Pentecostal churches are baptizing people into the faith by the millions every year and are on the frontlines of many of the social issues in our world today. They are battling AIDS, alleviating poverty and hunger, providing resources for addiction recovery, and more.

Some of the criticism may be a reaction against the fact that many high-profile charismatic and Pentecostal leaders have left mainline denominations. Several successful ministers, such as John Osteen, James Robison, and Pat Robertson, were ordained Southern Baptist ministers before openly embracing the baptism of the Holy Spirit. Dwight McKissic, prominent Southern Baptist pastor and member of the board at Southwestern Seminary in Fort Worth, Texas, openly encourages speaking in tongues and acknowledges that a certain prejudice exists.

> Many in the S.B.C. (Southern Baptist Convention) do not want to accept the inerrant Word of God when it comes to praying in tongues. They see it as irrational, but faith is irrational. I think they have chosen to reject it rather than teach it as God's word.[173]

Yet there are signs that this debate is softening. The once rigidly fundamentalist Dallas Theological Seminary has recently done away with restrictions on speaking in tongues for students and staff. That decision came only a few years after one of the seminary's prominent professors left the institution after having had a full gospel experience. That professor, Jack Deere, described his experience and wrote a passionate biblical defense of the charismatic movement in his books *Surprised by the Power of the Spirit* and *Surprised by the Voice of God*.

T. D. JAKES AND THE CIVIL RIGHTS MOVEMENT

In November 2005, Rosa Parks, the Civil Rights movement icon who refused to move to the back of a Birmingham bus, passed away. At the time, many were lamenting that perhaps the entire movement had died with her. Parks' funeral was attended by the full roster of today's civil rights leaders and activists. There were politicians like Congressmen John Dingell and Danny Davis, as well as Senator Barack Obama. Of course, white politicians were there, too, such as Bill and Hillary Clinton, John Kerry, and Michigan Governor Jennifer Granholm. Aretha Franklin sang a powerful solo, and among the speakers was Bernice King, one of the four children of Martin Luther King. The service lasted for seven hours. As Jesse Jackson reminded those gathered, "Some people's lives are worthy of taking the time to say good-bye." Sitting directly next to Jackson was T. D. Jakes.

Despite Jakes's tireless work at the emotional healing of his local community, as well as his financial investments in it, there are leaders within the black community who have questioned Jakes's devotion to the cause. A *Washington Post* article quoted two of his critics. One was Cain Hope Felder, dean of the Howard University Divinity School: "He never speaks on racism. He never speaks on the brutality of the criminal justice system."[174] Another voice with similar sentiments was Eugene Rivers, a pastor and community activist from Boston.

> Is he any different from the football player from Louisiana who's got the diamond stud? Or the rapper from South Central who made good?...T. D. Jakes is a great teacher and motivational speaker. As to his moral, theological legacy, the jury's out....Fifteen years from now, what difference will this have made beyond making Bishop Jakes a very wealthy man?[175]

Then the *Post* offered its own response:

Jakes does not find this a difficult question to answer. The difference lies in every homeless person his church bathes and feeds, every mother counseled, and prisoner given hope. If, in doing that, Jakes builds an empire that seems as much about self-promotion as the word of God, maybe that's a fair trade-off.

Jakes has been one of the few African-American leaders to articulate the contrasts and contradictions that can exist when one has to balance following Christ with following a political agenda:

On the moral issues, I think African-Americans tend to be conservative. However, if we line up—and I've worked very diligently to explain this to right-wing Christians—if we line up with our theological views, we do it at the expense often of our sociological needs in our community. If we line up with our sociological needs, we do it often at the expense of our moral convictions. Tragically, this generation has limited its definition of morality to two issues: same-sex marriages and abortion. Morality goes far beyond those two issues. Racism is immoral. I think racial profiling is immoral. I think not providing health care is immoral. To let someone die in a country that is as progressive as ours for the lack of something that is within our power to give them is immoral. It is virtually murder.[176]

ABANDONING THE MESSAGE OF KING

The most recent controversy thrust upon Jakes came from a 2008 CNN commentary recognizing the fortieth anniversary of Martin Luther King's assassination. The commentary basically accused many in the black church of having abandoned the message and legacy of Dr. King and instead having adopted the message of prosperity. It said,

[Black preachers and scholars say] King's "prophetic" model of ministry—one that confronted political and economic institutions of power—has been sidelined by the prosperity gospel.

Prosperity ministers preach that God rewards the faithful with wealth and spiritual power. Prosperity pastors such as Bishop T. D. Jakes have become the most popular preachers in the black church. They've also become brands. They've built megachurches and business empires with the prosperity message.[177]

For his part, Jakes was deeply offended. Usually he ignores public criticism as not worth his time for a response. This time, perhaps due to the invoking of King's legacy and the prominence of CNN, he wanted to answer the criticism, and the cable network allowed Jakes to write a response.

> Not only have I long been inspired by King's teachings, I remain inspired by his messages and have used them as a foundation for so many of the programs our church has instituted, including but not limited to: our prison outreach program, our Texas Offenders Reentry Initiative, as well as our continued and highly noted work with HIV/AIDS.
>
> Our commitment to education, with the opening of a $14 million college prep school, Clay Academy, has prompted praise....
>
> Other examples of our work include economic development programs as well as our tireless efforts for victims of Hurricane Katrina, which resulted in placing more than 2,000 survivors in homes.
>
> Internationally, not only does our church build water wells in Africa, but it also has provided computer technology in Kenya and has partnered with Church World Service, Habitat for Humanity, World Vision, and the Red Cross....
>
> Many people can talk the talk of King and his messages, but there are many who choose to focus on walking the walk. We walk the walk.[178]

WORKING TOGETHER

In recent years, there seems to be a refreshing and welcome cry for Christians to set aside differences, or at least to agree to disagree, so that we might all focus on the task at hand: proclaiming the gospel. There seems to be an emerging realization that all of our internal squabbles about doctrine and practice, which at times can become exceedingly ugly and vicious, do nothing to communicate the love of God to a watching world. Calvinists and Armenians need to work together. Pre- and post-rapture believers can both worship the Lord. White, black, brown, and every other shade of God's people need to work in harmony to prove that, while there are issues on which good Christian people will disagree, we must continue to rise above the strife, fellowship together, and proclaim God's love to a world that so badly needs it.

WEALTH AND AFFLUENCE

It's kind of an old horse that's been beaten to death for me. Most people understand that anybody who has sold seven million books can afford a house and a suit.

—T. D. Jakes[179]

Ministry is completely different in the African-American community. The church is everything. We've never had a president, we've only had preachers. So when we look to the preacher, he's the president. Many of us have not had fathers, so he's the daddy we didn't have. We take pride in him in a way white folks don't understand.

—T. D. Jakes

Chapter Twelve

WEALTH AND AFFLUENCE

T. D. Jakes has always done what comes naturally. From preaching to motivational speaking to counseling to writing books to building the ministry, Jakes did not rely on formal training or postgraduate degrees; he just did it. As noted earlier in this book, he did not come from wealth and privilege, but he did come from a family of entrepreneurs.

Before a long and fatal illness changed his fortunes, Jakes's father built a successful business from the ground up. Odith Jakes owned rental properties and created additional income from speaking to civic groups and other gatherings. Both of Jakes's grandmothers worked and created businesses that provided for their families. From his earliest days, Jakes worked at anything that could earn him a few dollars, whether it was selling vegetables from the garden or Avon products to ladies in the neighborhood. Later, he ran his father's business. T. D. Jakes has always been a hardworking man. At a tender age, he was forced to assume adult responsibilities, and it has impacted his entire life. Jakes has taken his drive and turned it into a ministry and business empire.

From the time his ministry began to explode on a national level, Jakes organized everything from a business perspective. He created separate and distinct organizations so there would be well-established lines between them. He didn't want any confusion regarding his roles as pastor, outside ministry coordinator, and businessman.

As we have seen, first, there was the church where Jakes preached, led services, and cared for his congregation. Then there was T. D. Jakes Ministries, a nonprofit organization that coordinated the radio and television ministry as well as conferences such as The Pastors and Leadership Conference, ManPower, and Woman, Thou Art Loosed. Later, TDJM also coordinated the massive amount of work necessary to pull off MegaFest in Atlanta. Finally, Jakes established T. D. Jakes Enterprises, a for-profit organization, to coordinate his books and plays, as well as music and movie productions. These were riskier projects that required a great deal more capital to produce. It has been T. D. Jakes Enterprises that has created the personal cash flow for Jakes and his family. He easily earns a seven- and quite possibly eight-figure annual income, all of it created apart from any potential salaries from his church and ministry.

> Jakes has always been a hardworking man. He has taken his drive and turned it into a ministry and a business empire.

Speak to T. D. Jakes in the middle of his day and you will hear him talk of "being on the clock." In his mind, he is punching a time clock where he must achieve a certain level of productivity before he is able to punch out and go home. His mind is always working to find a way to make the most of what the Lord has given him. He is continually striving to take the books he has written and the music he has recorded and do more with them. He is always looking for new themes and subject matter that will feed people's souls as well as teach them to do more with what the Lord has given them.

QUESTIONS ABOUT LIFESTYLE

Some in the secular world, as well as many in the Christian world, seem to be confused about or even resentful of Jakes's lifestyle. It looks unseemly to them that a pastor should become so prosperous. There must be something wrong or unethical occurring. Some watchdog groups have criticized Jakes for not making his ministry's financial information public. Ole Anthony, president of the Trinity Foundation, a Dallas-based religious watchdog group, has stated that there's never been any hint of fraud in Jakes's ministry. Despite this, even Anthony cringes at Jakes's lifestyle. "I excuse him a little bit because he grew up dirt-poor; hopefully he'll grow out of it."[180]

Criticism regarding Jakes's income and how he chooses to spend it began even before he moved to Dallas. The *Dallas Observer* reported,

> His conferences draw tens of thousands. His television show, broadcast on both the Trinity Broadcasting Network and Black Entertainment Television, reaches hundreds of thousands. He has spawned his own industry, T. D. Jakes Ministries, which sells his books—10 in all, with five best-sellers—and videotapes, the income from which allowed him to spend nearly 1 million last year on a residence in his hometown of Charleston, West Virginia.[181]

In addition to the level of income, however, the magazine seemed to be put off by Jakes's lack of shame about his lifestyle.

> He says he is not embarrassed by this, even if his extravagant lifestyle has caused controversy in his hometown that will likely follow him to Dallas. His suits are tailored. He drives a brand-new Mercedes. Both he and his wife Serita are routinely decked out in stunning jewelry. His West Virginia residence—two homes side by side—includes an indoor swimming pool and a bowling alley. These two homes particularly cause the ire of the local folks. One paper wrote in length about the purchase and made much of their unusual features. A columnist dubbed Jakes a "huckster."[182]

Jakes has his own response for those who question his wealth and lifestyle.

> I often ask people, "If you were interviewing Patricia Cornwell or Tom Clancy, would you ask about their house?" People generally say, "No". Well, they are top writers at Penguin Putnam, and I'm a best-selling author there as well....Now what's different is I'm African-American and I'm clergy. Which one of these differences should make me not get paid for my work?[183]

Even those who appreciate Jakes's message and powerful ministry are sometimes troubled by the "disconnect" projected by the mansion, fancy suits, and private jet. One is Shayne Lee, an Oral Roberts University graduate who is now a sociology professor at the University of Houston. On one hand, Lee says, "His message is uplifting and encouraging. It's postmodern therapy. He's incredible in how he's able to diagnose people's pain. He has an uncanny ability to put a finger on the human condition."[184] On the other hand, Lee admits, "He's a walking contradiction between compassion and arrant capitalism."[185] Lee wrote an unauthorized biography of Jakes in 2005.

In an interview with *Ebony*, Jakes was asked to respond to the critics of his lifestyle and his habit of traveling first class.

> No other movie producer or record label owner would be called upon to defend the quality of his clothes or the stature of his home. Additionally, the vast majority of the well-informed realize that any author who has 7 million books sold to his credit need not justify his enjoyment of some level of success as a reflection of his life's work. Unfortunately, people often limit preachers to one vocation while they themselves enjoy several. I chose not to allow my faith to restrict me from my for-profit entrepreneurial pursuits. I am proud to be one of Penguin Putnam's top three authors and to be the only African-American so distinguished.[186]

CULTURAL DIFFERENCES

It is interesting to see how the issues of wealth and lifestyle quickly highlight differences between white and black churches in America. The *Dallas Observer* article ended by suggesting that Jakes's take on wealth may be influenced in part by his belief that Jesus Himself may well have been a wealthy Christian. As the article stated,

> Jesus "employed" twelve people to help spread his message, Jakes says, as though the apostles were on salary....Jakes asks, "Why else would Roman soldiers have gambled for his cloak as Jesus lay dying on the cross, if the cloak hadn't been unusually valuable?"

> The espousal of a rich Jesus isn't new: It's a theory that has gained some currency among black Pentecostals. And although it may seem wild to white onlookers, it underscores a very basic difference between the attitudes of blacks and whites when it comes to their ministers' financial fates.

> It is the white Christian tradition...that those who undertake the work of God should require nothing in exchange beyond bare subsistence and the satisfaction of sacrifice. African-American Pentecostals, however, look upon poverty as a spiritual curse. They believe that those who serve the Lord will receive greater prosperity.[187]

Admittedly, some of the confusion likely stems from the racially segregated nature of American Christianity and the lack of understanding that exists between the white and black churches. For instance, it is not unusual in African-American churches for the pastor to wear the nicest clothes in the congregation and to drive the nicest car. This practice does not create controversy in these congregations. In fact, the material well-being of a pastor is often viewed as a reflection of the success of the congregation in that they are able to take care of their pastor as he faithfully pursues the ministry to which God has called him.

Whites often underestimate the expectations put on black pastors to do their best to pull the African-American community up out of its struggling economic condition. Having been raised in poverty, Jakes knows how African-Americans have been told by politicians that their future is tied to welfare payments rather than to becoming self-supporting business owners. Thus, Jakes's message has always been that if blacks want to receive the full blessings of God on their lives, they should seek to become educated and entrepreneurial, and to accumulate wealth that can be passed down to the generations that will follow after them.

In a 2007 sermon, Jakes shared how the welfare system is not merely a political issue, but also a spiritual one:

> The reason welfare never works is because welfare was never meant to be permanent. It was meant to sustain you through a particular period of adversity so you could launch from that into a sustained period of blessing where you're not always waiting for someone to shake your hand. Because if you have to live off of people shaking your hand, you become a beggar in the kingdom, and you start manipulating people because you need them to shake your hand to make it. And that is not God's will.[188]

Jakes goes beyond the usual prosperity verses that suggest that God wants His followers to be financially and materially blessed. He preaches that people have a responsibility to themselves, their families, and their God to do the most they can with their lives in every way. He encourages his congregation to earn money, build a nest egg, and buy nice clothes if that's how they want to spend their disposable income. He says,

> I have to talk about economic empowerment because it is a reality for my people. Pastor Joe Success at First Suburban Christian Church does not need to preach that message. But I am preaching to men who get out of prison and can't get a job and can't feed

their families. They can confess Jesus in their heart, and that's great, but they've got four kids by two different women and their choices are to deal drugs or work at Burger King.[189]

He uses similar terms when defending his own lifestyle, suggesting that black working-class men and women need...

...believable heroes; we don't need preachers who've taken vows of poverty or who, on the other extreme, are living out of the offering plate. We need a preacher who, through writing or some other honest means, has made the American dream work for him. The American dream has been our nightmare.[190]

He often refers to how the black church needs to be free and unashamed to be itself.

We need to know that it can be done—economically, spiritually, maritally...by flawed and broken people. Churches that pretend to be full of perfect people will turn [African-Americans] off. That kind of stuff estranges our people because they cannot relate to it. They think, "Oh, I'm ineligible for this; I can't do this," and they go to something else, be it drugs or the Nation of Islam or a soap opera or a string of lovers.[191]

In addition to Bible verses and words of faith and hope, Jakes mixes in the practical. In a 2004 *Ebony* article, he encouraged readers to become fiscally accountable:

Many people can be publicly successful and privately complete failures. Many people spend hundreds of dollars on the latest imported suit and fine-skin shoes, only to struggle to scrape together the money needed to keep the lights from being cut off or the eviction notice from being delivered.[192]

Jakes sees the responsibility of encouraging his people to change their financial situations as crucial to his ministry. In his book *Maximize the Moment*, he wrote about creating a life plan. He admitted that Christians often think that walking by faith means having no goals but simply waiting for God to drop a fully formed plan in their laps. If faith means having what you hope for, however, then Jakes believes that people must have some idea of what they are hoping for. Throughout the book, he laid the groundwork for life principles that will help people reach the goals they have established in their life plans.

In *The Great Investment*, Jakes wrote of how he had seen people go from total poverty to abundance—he and Serita had experienced it firsthand. He also wrote of the many people over the years who have equated poverty with righteousness. He stressed that poverty builds character, but it does not equal godliness. Jakes believes that it is not God's plan for His people to live lives of financial desperation. At the same time, he teaches that materialism should not be the goal of life. The goal is balance.

> Jakes stressed that poverty builds character, but it does not equal godliness. It is not God's plan for His people to live lives of financial desperation.

He recalled witnessing to Africans whose idea of wealth was a goat. For Jakes, the goal of life is to have an adequate amount to make us content with life. Through his Web site, Jakes offers articles free of charge with such titles as "How to Fix Your Credit," "Free Legal Advice as You Start Your Business," and "What You Need to Know about Paying for College"—all written by experts in their fields.

In truth, Jakes's sermons are not filled with the "name it and claim it," "gab it and grab it," prosperity theology that many evangelicals love to criticize. Jakes seems to be a man on a mission to help all people, but particularly African-Americans, to refuse to become victims and instead become masters of their own financial fates while holding on to responsibility and following godly principles. He understands that circumstances sometimes dictate that we accept whatever assistance we can find to make it from absolute desperation to a place where the future is brighter. Jakes has been through the desperate times and now he is an example of what can happen if one keeps doing the right thing in the midst of the struggle.

When Jakes stands in front of his congregation in his tailored suits and gold cuff links, and when Serita joins him dressed in a beautiful matching outfit, his congregation, for the most part, does not view them as grabbing all they can to live the high life. They are seen primarily as a couple who conquered life's struggles and came out on top. They worked together when the utilities were being cut off and there was no food in the house, and through their faith in God's provision and their hard work, they now live in luxury and are able do what they want with their lives. To many African-Americans, T. D. and Serita Jakes are an example of what is possible when people follow Christian principles and succeed.

Jakes's approach is unique in Christian churches, particularly compared with other megachurches. There are many who preach that being faithful to the Lord in respect to tithes and offerings will directly result in God's blessings. There are other churches that teach about the importance of budgeting and other life skills. Jakes's mission, however, seems to be educating his people about taking the 90 percent that remains after the tithe and using it to provide a financial foundation that will not only bless their families today, but also provide an underpinning for generations yet to come. Some will argue that the church's mission should be limited to establishing a path to *spiritual* prosperity only, not *financial* prosperity. Jakes believes that the African-American community needs God's help in this life—not just in the one to come.

In 2001, a study reported a startling statistic: there were 603,000 African-American men in college, but there were 791,000 in prison.[193]

This ongoing situation is having a major impact on many families within the African-American community who have lost earning power and family stability due to the absence of these men in their lives. This crisis has led to other problems in the African-American community, such as prostitution, drug abuse, child abandonment, and a significantly higher rate of unemployment. These combined factors mean that a smaller percentage of African-American families are able to purchase homes, save for retirement, and help the next generation obtain the education necessary to climb the ladder of success.

Jakes attacks this problem head-on. He admits that prejudice and discrimination still exist, and that African-Americans cannot necessarily change the world around them. Yet they *can* refuse to allow such things to stop them from achieving their goals. Instead, they should use these realities as motivation to become all they can be. They must show those who are racist and ignorant that their attitudes cannot and will not prevail. Attitudes cannot always be changed, but they can be overcome.

> African-Americans cannot necessarily change the world around them, yet they *can* refuse to allow such things to stop them from achieving their goals.

This concept is the theme of Jakes's latest book, *Reposition Yourself: Living Life without Limits*, in which he defines success in life, discusses how people can place themselves in a position to achieve the goals they set, and warns them never to let anything stand in the way of achieving their dreams. He writes of the glass ceiling that blocks many women from reaching their goals. He acknowledges that there are roadblocks in life and that achieving a goal is rarely easy. Therefore, he warns readers that the goals they set will often have a high price. He also encourages people not to be so dedicated to achieving goals that they leave others behind. There is a balance between driving to achieve goals and paying respect to the price others have paid to make it all possible.

T. D. knows that he has a large number of women and minorities in his congregation, and he wants to do everything he can to encourage them to take the steps necessary to change their lives economically as well as spiritually. He claims that the wealth of the African-American community could be equal to the economy of the eleventh largest country in the world. He talks about how people often make wrong decisions that sentence them to a life of poverty. Too much money, Jakes says, is spent on rent, cars, fur coats, or other things that depreciate. Achieving wealth, Jakes says, can often be attributed to sticking to simple financial principles, such as compound interest, that have been known for centuries. He tells his congregation that some people are aware of these principles and follow them and that is why they achieve wealth while others remain in poverty.

Whether Jakes's personal wealth is a hindrance or help to his ministry is debatable, but he certainly has been an inspiration to both African-Americans and women throughout this country and in other nations of the world. He is making a difference in people's lives by providing practical advice on basic household budgeting, saving, and investing. By doing this, Jakes is striving to achieve what many government programs have failed to do.

THE WORLD IS HIS PARISH

I am grateful that God has allowed me to discover some talents and resources. Aside from ministry and aside from preaching, I have been able to explore creativity, open up businesses, and still be true to my calling. I am willing to use every platform I have—from the pulpit to the pen to the play—to inform our people about the choices they have, to empower them.

—T. D. Jakes[194]

Chapter Thirteen

THE WORLD IS HIS PARISH

O n one of the most fateful days in American history, T. D. Jakes was on the cover of one of America's most prestigious magazines. Released on September 10, 2001, one day before planes hit the World Trade Center and the Pentagon, *Time* magazine's theme was "America's Best." Jakes's picture graced the cover above the words, "Is This Man the Next Billy Graham?"

The article described Jakes's Pentecostal style of preaching, which it compared to the acting of Marlon Brando and the basketball skills of Michael Jordan. It stated, "He purrs like Isaac Hayes and screams like Jay Hawkins."[195]

Jakes's name and reputation have begun to be mentioned in the same breath as the late Dr. Martin Luther King Jr. and other giants of the civil rights movement. Although Jakes's profile does not match those of other civil rights leaders, he has gained a respect in the African-American community that few can match, past or present.

HURRICANE KATRINA

Like Dr. King, Jakes has avoided showing favoritism to either national political party and has been called upon to advise Democrats and Republicans alike. In the summer of 2005, Jakes was once again called by the White House to be a national leader. After the destruction of New Orleans in the wake of Hurricane Katrina, there was a loss of faith in the government by African-Americans all over the country, particularly in the areas afflicted by the storm. President Bush asked Jakes to help oversee government programs that would assist in distributing approximately twenty million dollars of the one hundred and ten million dollars raised by former presidents George H. W. Bush and Bill Clinton.

Jakes did not take the White House request lightly. He met with relief organizations and local religious leaders to discuss the best way to help the victims. He and the Reverend William H. Gray III, former president of the United Negro College Fund, were named as cochairs of a nine-member, multi-faith committee charged with disbursing funds to churches destroyed by the storm.

> Jakes has been through the desperate times and now he is an example of what can happen if one keeps doing the right thing in the midst of the struggle.

The Potter's House also reached out to help the affected region. Within two days of the hurricane, they established a telephone bank to field calls from people trying to make contact with the government and charitable organizations. They also distributed food, clothes, diapers, toiletries, and school supplies. The medical ministry filled prescriptions to provide blood pressure, heart, and diabetes medications. In partnership with the World Children's Fund, they donated 250,000 dollars' worth of meals, nutrition bars, water, ice, and first aid—about two hundred tons of materials. They also raised thousands of dollars through a free benefit concert featuring some of the most popular names in gospel music.

Initially the White House-appointed committee assumed it would be giving about five hundred grants of $35,000 each. But as the applications began trickling in, the committee realized that there were far fewer applications than had been anticipated. In consultation with the cochairs of the fund, the grant ceiling was raised to $100,000. After this there were disagreements among various government agencies with overlapping jurisdictions. Without consulting the committee, government staffers cut checks to thirty-eight churches for $35,000 each. It had been agreed previously by everyone that audits would be conducted to ensure that these churches did in fact exist, but no audits were ever conducted. The committee also never received any funds from the money raised by the former presidents.

A few months after he had assumed this responsibility, Jakes resigned, stating that the government was not consulting with them regarding disbursement of the funds but merely acting as it saw fit. In Jakes's mind, the government had given its word and then broken it. He was quoted as saying, "I've been in ministry for thirty years and I don't think I've ever resigned from anything. I'm a loyalist to a fault. But what's happened is unacceptable."[196]

Some in the black press jumped on this inequity and proclaimed it to be racist, declaring that the promised funds were being withheld because they were designated to help African-American families and faith groups. "T. D. Jakes has not gotten his $20 million Katrina check because the corporate rulers have no intention of allowing blacks from New Orleans to regroup and return."[197]

Despite the controversy, the fact that T. D. Jakes was asked to serve on a committee with such a national exposure attests to his leadership status in the nation.

OTHER RECOGNITIONS

T. D. Jakes continues to be recognized by groups and organizations across the country as one of the most prominent pastors and Christian leaders in the country. In March 2004, he was presented with the President's Award during the 35th NAACP Image Awards. The President's Award is presented to individuals exemplifying high standards of character, conviction, and achievement. When the announcement was made, NAACP president Kweisi Mfume said,

> Bishop Thomas D. Jakes has been called the "Shepherd to the Shattered," as he reaches out to the poor and the rich, the young and old, those behind bars, those in the classroom, people in the inner city, and people in the suburbs. From The Potter's House in Dallas, Texas, he preaches to people of all colors and ethnicities. He is more than a preacher. He is a community advocate, humanitarian, author, songwriter, playwright, conference speaker, and broadcaster. I can think of no one who more epitomizes what the NAACP Image Awards represent and who is more than deserving of receiving this year's President's Award."[198]

Jakes continues to be introduced by members of the secular press as "America's most influential pastor." When Oprah Winfrey invites Jakes to her stage, she welcomes him as a friend and fellow leader in the African-American community. She has invested portions of her personal wealth in his projects and knows him to be a man who strives to make a difference in his life and community.

DOING WHAT HE MUST DO

The people of The Potter's House of Dallas know they must share their pastor with the world. There are many times when he is not in the pulpit due to his frequent travel. On Mother's Day 2007, the first lady of the congregation, Serita, was in the pulpit and announced to the congregation, "The Bishop is away doing what he must do. We all know that the Bishop is too big to be held down to one local church."

Over two centuries ago, John Wesley said, "The world is my parish." Because Wesley believed this to be his mission, through his efforts and the efforts of those who followed his leadership, he made a major impact on the eighteenth century world around him. The world is T. D. Jakes's parish as well. Whether through preaching, conferences, radio and TV, the Internet, books, plays, music, or movies, Jakes has used every tool at his disposal, and some that others never imagined, to touch the world—his parish.

Jakes seems to understand the responsibility he has as America's preacher to craft sermons that will allow his parishioners around the world to gain the faith they need to turn to God and become the people that He created them to be. Despite the constant critics who pass judgment on his words and deeds, T. D. Jakes realizes the gravity of his calling and simply keeps preaching, sure of who he is and the message God has given him.

ENDNOTES

1 Tim Rogers, "30 People We Love," *D Magazine*, October 2004.

2 David Van Biema, "Spirit Raiser," *Time*, September 17, 2001.

3 T. D. Jakes, *Mama Made the Difference* (New York: Putnam Adult, 2006), 37.

4 T. D. Jakes, *Daddy Loves His Little Girls* (Lake Mary, FL: Charisma House, 1996) 82–83.

5 T. D. Jakes, "Vessels of Mercy," address, Woman, Thou Art Loosed Conference, Tampa, August 1997.

6 Deborah Caldwell, "Why T. D. Jakes Stays Christian," Beliefnet.com, June 2005. http://www.beliefnet.com/story/167/story_16716_1.html.

7 T. D. Jakes interview by Leon Harris, "America's Best in Society and Culture," CNN, September 9, 2001.

8 Libby Copeland, "With Gifts from God," *Washington Post*, March 25, 2001.

9 T. D. Jakes, *Follow the Star: Christmas Stories That Changed My Life* (New York: Berkeley Publishing Group, 2003), 32.

10 John Blake, "Therapy and Theology: Atlanta's MegaFest Shows Many Sides of T. D. Jakes's Ministry," *Atlanta Journal-Constitution*, June 23, 2004.

11 William Martin, "American Idol," *Texas Monthly*, August 2006.

12 T. D. Jakes, "Grateful Leaders Fill Empty Pew," *Ministries Today*, January/February 1998.

13 T. D. Jakes, *Lay Aside the Weight* (Minneapolis: Bethany House Publishers, 1997), 17.

14 Teresa Hairston, "30 Years of Vision and Victory," *Gospel Today*, May/June 2004.

15 Copeland, "With Gifts from God."

16 T. D. Jakes, *Maximize the Moment* (New York: G. P. Putnam's Sons, 1999), 174.

17 Henry Kaylois, "Bishop Jakes Is Ready. Are You?" *Dallas Observer*, June 20, 1996.

18   Vanessa E. Jones, "T. D. Jakes Lets Loose with His Film about Child Sexual Abuse, the Preacher Takes His Message Nationwide," *Boston Globe*, October 21, 2004.

19   Kaylois, "Bishop Jakes Is Ready. Are You?"

20   Ibid.

21   Hazel Trice Edney, "Bishop T.D. Jakes Surprises Himself," National Newspaper Publishers Association (NNPA), BlackPressUSA, January 10, 2005. http://www.blackpressusa.com/news/Article.asp?SID=3&Title=National+News&NewsID=3620.

22   T. D. Jakes, *Can You Stand to Be Blessed?* (Shippensburg, PA: Treasure House, 1994), 84.

23   Rogers, "T.D. Jakes."

24   Kaylois, "Bishop Jakes Is Ready. Are You?"

25   Kelly Starling, "Why People, Especially Black Women, are Talking about Bishop T. D. Jakes," *Ebony*, January 1, 2001.

26   Berta Delgado, "T.D. Jakes: With New Film, Bishop Jakes' Reach Extends Even Further," *Dallas Morning News*, September 25, 2004.

27   "Preacher Offers Solace to Shattered Souls," http://www.cnn.com/SPECIALS/2001/americasbest/TIME/society.culture/pro.tdjakes.html.

28   Ibid.

29   Sridhar Pappu, "The Preacher," *Atlantic Monthly*, March 2006.

30   T. D. Jakes, "It's Just Life," *The Potter's Touch*, August 21, 2007.

31   Jakes, *Can You Stand to Be Blessed?* 20–22.

32   Serita Ann Jakes, *Beside Every Good Man* (New York: Warner Faith, 2003), 126.

33   Copeland, "With Gifts from God."

34   Ibid.

35   Jakes, *Daddy Loves His Little Girls*, 15–17.

36   Cathy Lynn Grossman, "T. D. Jakes: Spiritual Salesman," *USA Today*, December 27, 2000.

37   Jakes, *Maximize the Moment*, 41–42.

38   Kaylois, "Bishop Jakes Is Ready. Are You?"

39   Lynell George, "Jakes Fits 2 Worlds Under His Tent," tdjakes.com, July 19, 2002. http://www.tdjakes.com/site/News2?page=NewsArticle&id=5161.

40 Starling, "Why People, Especially Black Women, are Talking about Bishop T. D. Jakes."

41 Tim Madigan, "T. D. Jakes: Self made with God's help," *Orlando Sentinel*, June 11, 2006.

42 Michael Duduit, "Preaching to Mend Broken Lives: An interview with T. D. Jakes," *Preaching*, http://www.preaching.com/resources/features/11545843.

43 Starling, "Why People, Especially Black Women, Are Talking about Bishop T. D. Jakes."

44 Leon Harris, interviewing T. D. Jakes, "America's Best in Society and Culture."

45 T. D. Jakes, *God's Leading Lady* (New York: Berkley Books, 2002), 18.

46 Pappu, "The Preacher."

47 Annette John-Hall, "T. D. Jakes: Building an Empire to Empower," *Philadelphia Inquirer*, August 22, 2005.

48 Sam Wellman, *T. D. Jakes* (Philadelphia: Chelsea House Publishers, 2000), 66.

49 Kaylois, "Bishop Jakes Is Ready. Are You?"

50 Jakes, *Daddy Loves His Little Girls*, 104.

51 John-Hall, "T. D. Jakes: Building an Empire to Empower."

52 Wellman, *T. D. Jakes*, 69.

53 Rogers, "T.D. Jakes."

54 Ibid.

55 Starling, "Why People, Especially Black Women, Are Talking about Bishop T. D. Jakes."

56 John-Hall, "T. D. Jakes: Building an Empire to Empower."

57 Don Wray, "Ministry Watch.com's Take," November 2003, http://www.ministrywatch.com/mw2.1/F_SumRpt.asp?EIN=311506712.

58 Ibid.

59 Starling, "Why People, Especially Black Women, Are Talking about Bishop T. D. Jakes."

60 Ibid.

61 Tim Madigan, "Evangelist's Flock Growing," *Deseret Morning News*, February 4, 2000.

62 Ibid.

63   "Weakening the Wall: Al Gore Grovels for Votes with Promise Keeper T. D. Jakes," American Atheists, Inc., October 25, 2000, http://www.atheists.org/flash.line/elec20.htm.

64   Jim Jones, "T. D. Jakes Plays Himself in Movie Based on His Book," *Fort Worth Star-Telegram*, July 31, 2004.

65   "Weakening the Wall," http://www.atheists.org/flash.line/elec20.htm.

66   Julie Fairchild, "High-Tech Holy Ground," *Ministries Today*, September/October 2000.

67   Kevin Sack, "In a Texas Church, Gore Campaigns for Morality, Values and 'Prosperity of the Spirit'," *New York Times*, October 23, 2000.

68   Lauren Winner, "T. D. Jakes Feels Your Pain," *Christianity Today*, February 7, 2000.

69   http://www.outreachmagazine.com/docs/top100_2004.pdf.

70   http://www.outreachmagazine.com/docs/top100_2005.pdf.

71   http://www.outreachmagazine.com/docs/top100_2006.pdf.

72   http://www.outreachmagazine.com/docs/top100_2007_fastest.pdf.

73   Dr. John N. Vaughan, "Top 50 Most Influential Churches," *The Church Report*, January 2006.

74   Dahleen Glanton, "When T. D. Jakes Speaks…," *Today's Christian*, February 2005.

75   Grossman, "T. D. Jakes: Spiritual Salesman."

76   Tony Carnes, "Bush's Defining Moment," *Christianity Today*, November 12, 2001.

77   T. D. Jakes, "Awake from Your Slumber," Beliefnet.com, http://www.beliefnet.com/story/88/story_8804_1.html.

78   "The 25 Most Influential Evangelists in America," *Time*, January 30, 2005, http://www.time.com/time/covers/1101050207/photoessay/13.html.

79   Elisabeth Bumiller, "White House Letters: Politics and prayer mix in post-Katrina sermon," *International Herald Tribune*, September 18, 2005.

80   Ibid.

81   Hazel Trice Edney, "Bishop T. D. Jakes 'Sick' Over Slow Response to Katrina," *Louisiana Weekly*, September 26, 2005.

82   Kevin Eigelbach, "Bishop: We Must Preach against Racism," *Cincinnati Post*, June 13, 2003.

Endnotes

83   Edney, "Bishop T. D. Jakes Surprises Himself."

84   T. D. Jakes, "No Political Party Can Contain Us," CNN, October 20, 2006, http://www.cnn.com/2006/US/07/05/jakes.commentary/.

85   Edney, "Bishop T. D. Jakes Surprises Himself."

86   Diane Weathers, "Bishop T. D. Jakes: On the power of family," tdjakes.com, December 1, 2001. http://www.tdjakes.com/site/News2?page=NewsArticle&id=5165.

87   Victoria Lynn Childress, "Celebrating the Journey," *The Potter's House Times*, Summer 2007.

88   Sam Hodges, "Ready for His Close-Up?" *Dallas Morning News*, January 21, 2006.

89   Jakes, *Mama Made the Difference*, 71–72.

90   Jakes, *Mama Made the Difference*, 194.

91   T. D. Jakes, *The Lady, Her Lover, and Her Lord* (New York: G. P. Putnam's Sons, 1998), 191.

92   Jakes, *Mama Made the Difference*, 73.

93   Ibid, 69.

94   Richard Leiby, "Hollywood Reels In another Kingfish," *Washington Post*, January 6, 2005.

95   Nancy Lovell, "Home Is Where the Business Education Is," tdjakes.com, June 5, 2006, http://www.tdjakes.com/site/News2?page=NewsArticle&id=5585.

96   Ibid.

97   "The First Family of Megafest," *Gospel Today*, May/June 2005.

98   Lovell, "Home Is Where The Business Education Is."

99   Delgado, "T.D. Jakes: With new film, Bishop Jakes's reach extends even further."

100 John Blake, "Megafest Moment," *Atlanta Journal-Constitution*, July 20, 2006.

101 Tim Rogers, "30 People We Love," *D Magazine*, October, 2004.

102 Glanton, "When T. D. Jakes Speaks…."

103 T. D. Jakes interview on CNN, aired August 4, 2005.

104 T. D. Jakes, *Woman, Thou Art Loosed!* (Shippensburg, PA: Treasure House, 1993), 15.

105 Julie Salamon, "Preacher in a Star Turn on Film Draws the Faithful," *New York Times*, October 18, 2004.

106 LaTonya Taylor, "Jakes on the Loose," September 28, 2004. http://www.christianitytoday.com/movies/interviews/tdjakes.html.

107 Ira Hadnot, "T. D. Jakes Takes a Big Screen Leap," *Dallas Morning News*, September 26, 2004.

108 Jones, "T. D. Jakes Plays Himself in Movie Based on His Book."

109 Hadnot, "T. D. Jakes Takes a Big Screen Leap."

110 Taylor, "Jakes on the Loose," http://www.christianitytoday.com/movies/interviews/tdjakes.html.

111 Donna Britt, "T. D. Jakes: Pop culture slowly moves into the pew," *Washington Post*, September 24, 2004.

112 Ibid.

113 Salamon, "Preacher in a Star Turn on Film Draws the Faithful."

114 Jones, "T. D. Jakes Lets Loose."

115 T. D. Jakes, "Not Easily Produced," Bishop's Blog, tdjakes.com. http://tdjenterprises.com/blog/?p=14.

116 http://www.religionnews.com/press02/PRp21pp.html

117 http://www.tdjakes.com/site/PageServer?pagename=resrc_blog

118 Glanton, "When T. D. Jakes Speaks...."

119 "T. D. Jakes Enterprises Debuts Best Business Conferences," tdjakes.com, June 28, 2006, http://www.tdjakes.com/site/News2?page=NewsArticle&id=5695&news_iv_ctrl=1081.

120 T. D. Jakes, *So You Call Yourself a Man?* (New York: Inspirational Press, 2000), 278.

121 Berta Delgado, "Q & A with T. D," *Dallas Morning News*, May 21, 2004.

122 T. D. Jakes interview by *CNN Sunday Morning*, June 27, 2004.

123 "America's Favorite Preacher Hosts MegaFest 2005," *Gospel Today*, May 17, 2005.

124 Ibid.

125 Ibid.

126 Tracey Christensen, "Bishop Explains MegaFest Message," 11Alive.com (NBC affiliate WXIA-TV, Atlanta), http://www.11alive.com/news/article_news.aspx?storyid=67205.

127 Rhoda Tse, "MegaFest 2005: A total family experience," *Christian Post*, August 4, 2005.

[128] Valerie G. Lowe, "T. D. Jakes' MegaFest Event Draws 100,000," *Charisma*, October 2005.

[129] Rhoda Tse, "MegaFest Closes with Strengthened Families, Faith in Jesus," *Christian Post*, August 8, 2005.

[130] Ibid.

[131] Bo Emerson, "T. D. Jakes: What's the Draw for MegaFest?" *Atlanta Journal-Constitution*, August 5, 2005.

[132] Hazel Trice Edney, "Bishop Jakes and Black Press Vow to Support Each Other," NNPA, June 28, 2007.

[133] Maynard Eaton, "T. D. Jakes Decries 'Yellow Journalism'," *Atlanta Voice*, August 18, 2005.

[134] Maynard Eaton, "T. D. Jakes's MegaFest is 'Mega-Snub' to Black Press," *Atlanta Voice*, August 29, 2005.

[135] Ibid.

[136] Ibid.

[137] Ibid.

[138] Ibid.

[139] "For Men Only Conference and Retreat," Blacknews.com, February 24, 2006, http://www.mybrotha.com/tdjakes.asp.

[140] Clarence Waldron, "Bishop T. D. Jakes hosts Megafest 2006 in Atlanta; celebrates 30th anniversary in ministry," *Jet*, August 7, 2006.

[141] Ibid.

[142] The Potter's House, "Bishop T. D. Jakes' Official Statement Regarding MegaFest 2008," press release, July 3, 2007.

[143] Jakes, *God's Leading Lady*, 94.

[144] "Jakes Speaks Out on Africa," *Gospel Today*, May/June 2006.

[145] T. D. Jakes, "Draw It Out of Me!" sermon, Nairobi, Kenya, October 2, 2005.

[146] Suzanne C. Ryan, "New PBS Show Explores African-American Heritage in a New Way," *Boston Globe*, February 1, 2006.

[147] Edney, "Bishop T.D. Jakes Surprises Himself."

[148] Sonsyrea Tate, "T. D. Jakes Appreciates Connections to Africa," *Washington Informer*, September 14, 2006.

[149] Francis Ayieko, "How T. D. Jakes Manages to Mix Business with Preaching," *East African*, January 31, 2005.

150 Isaiah Mbuga, "T. D. Jakes Storms Kampala," *New Vision*, January 21, 2005.

151 Bishop T. D. Jakes and Andrew Young, "Don't Stop Caring for Africa," *District Chronicles*, August 4, 2005.

152 Ibid.

153 Agha Ibiam, "T. D. Jakes: a Message for Nigeria," *Asia Africa Intelligence Wire*, January 6, 2005.

154 Karen Borta, "From Texas to Africa, Part 2," KTVT-TV (CBS affiliate, Dallas, TX), February 17, 2005.

155 PR Newswire on behalf of The Potter's House of Dallas, "Faith for Africa: Bishop T. D. Jakes leads 300 African-Americans on humanitarian mission trip to Africa," press release, September 22, 2005.

156 Borta, "From Texas to Africa, Part 2."

157 http://www.blackwebportal.com/nuforums/vm.cfm?Forum=6&Topic=653.

158 "Bishop T. D. Jakes' Faith to Africa: Kenya mission increases aid with technology to East Africa," PR Newswire, October 4, 2006.

159 "Faith for Africa" (Kenya mission trip).

160 Church World Service, "Hotline: Kenya," http://www.churchworldservice.org/hotline/archives/2005/09-26-2005.html.

161 Ibid.

162 Jakes, "Draw It Out of Me!"

163 Robert Andrescik, "T. D. Jakes," *New Man*, November/December 2000.

164 T. D. Jakes, *Anointing Fall on Me* (Lanham, MD: Pneuma Life Publishing, 1997), 87.

165 Ted Olsen, "American Pentecost," *Christian History and Biography*, April 1, 1998.

166 International Center for Spiritual Renewal, "Azusa History," http://www.icfsr.org/history.html.

167 Martin, "American Idol."

168 T. D. Jakes, "My Views on the Godhead," *Christianity Today*, February 1, 2000.

169 Ibid.

170 Martin, "American Idol."

171 G. Richard Fisher, "'Get Ready' For T.D. Jakes: The Velcro Bishop with Another Gospel," Personal Freedom Outreach, 1997, http://www.pfo.org/jakes.html.

Endnotes

172 Kimberly Winston, "Speaking in Tongues: Faith's Language Barrier?" *USA Today*, May 23, 2007.

173 Ibid.

174 Copeland, "With Gifts from God."

175 Ibid.

176 Edney, "Bishop T.D. Jakes Surprises Himself."

177 John Blake, "Modern Black Church Shuns King's Message," CNN.com, April 4, 2006, http://www.cnn.com/2008/US/04/06/mlk.role.church/.

178 T. D. Jakes, "Church Walks the Walk of King's Message," CNN.com, April 14, 2008, http://www.cnn.com/2008/US/04/14/jakes/index.html.

179 CNN Interview: "CNN People in the News," with Fredricka Whitfield, December 25, 2004.

180 Delgado, "T.D. Jakes: With New Film, Bishop Jakes' Reach Extends Even Further."

181 Kaylois, "Bishop Jakes Is Ready. Are You?"

182 Ibid.

183 Jones, "T. D. Jakes Lets Loose."

184 Delgado, "T. D. Jakes: With New Film, Bishop Jakes' Reach Extends Even Further."

185 Ibid.

186 "5 Questions for: Bishop T.D. Jakes: Founder & Senior Pastor, The Potter's House," *Ebony*, December 4, 2004.

187 Delgado, "T.D. Jakes: With new film, Bishop Jakes's reach extends even further."

188 T. D. Jakes, "Favor Ain't Fair," sermon, The Potter's House, Dallas, TX, July 2007.

189 Winner, "T. D. Jakes Feels Your Pain."

190 Ibid.

191 Ibid.

192 T. D. Jakes, "How to Free Yourself Financially," *Ebony*, October 2004.

193 "Cellblocks or Classrooms?: The funding of higher education and corrections and its impact on African-American men," Justice Policy Institute, 2001, http://www.soros.org/initiatives/justice/articles_publications/publications/cellblocks_20020918.

[194] http://www.cnn.com/SPECIALS/2001/americasbest/TIME/society.culture/pro.tdjakes.html.

[195] Van Biema, "Spirit Raiser."

[196] Rukmini Callimachi, "Religious Leaders Quit Bush-Clinton Katrina Fund Panel," Associated Press, July 14, 2006.

[197] "Is T. D. Jakes Deal Going Sour?" Radio BC, *The Black Commentator*, March 9, 2006, http://www.blackcommentator.com/174/174_radio_bc/174_radio_bc_03_09_06_td_jake.html.

[198] http://www.naacpimageawards.net/media/imapresaward012204.html.

About the Author

Richard Young is a former educator, businessman, and pastor. The son of a Free Will Baptist pastor, Richard started preaching at fourteen and pastoring at twenty. He comes from a great heritage of preachers and pastors. There has been a member of his family in the ministry since 1876.

Richard received bachelor of arts and master of science degrees from Southern Nazarene University in Bethany, Oklahoma. He has completed the coursework for his doctorate in education at Oklahoma State University. He served as vice president of academics at American Christian College and Seminary in Oklahoma City as well as dean of academics at Oklahoma Junior College. He also was a trainer for Century 21 across the state of Oklahoma.

Richard has been a writer all of his adult life, writing corporate training manuals and collegiate self-study courses, as well as two textbooks. He has written articles for both Christian and secular magazines and journals. His previous book, *The Rise of Lakewood Church and Joel Osteen*, is also published by Whitaker House.

He and his wife Brenda, who have been married for over three and a half decades, have three children and nine grandchildren.

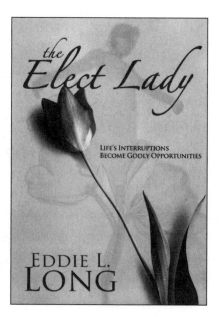

The Elect Lady:
Life's Interruptions Become Godly Opportunites
Eddie L. Long

Growing up, most little girls dream of loving husbands, beautiful homes, and perfect children. What happens when life doesn't turn out the way they expected?

To all the women who wonder what went wrong in their lives, Bishop Eddie Long brings this powerful message: Elect Lady, God sees your circumstances. The path to which He has called you may not be easy, but you are in the position to influence your children, your neighborhood, your church, and the world. *The Elect Lady*, a life-changing book written from the depths of Eddie Long's heart, will help you to receive God's best for your life, turn past mistakes into triumphs, recognize God's interruptions in your life as His divine direction, and discover that He has a better plan for you than you can imagine for yourself.

ISBN: 978-0-88368-281-4 • Hardcover • 192 pages

www.whitakerhouse.com

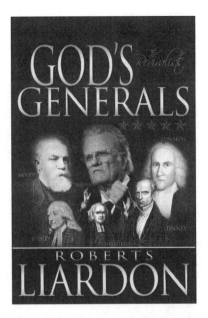

God's Generals: The Revivalists
Roberts Liardon

Roberts Liardon chronicles compelling spiritual biographies of some of the most powerful preachers ever to ignite the fires of revival. Follow the faith journeys and lives of the great generals of God, including: George Whitefield, whose dramatic flair and passionate preaching needed no modern conveniences like microphones to reach crowds of more than sixty thousand people; Charles Finney, the skeptical lawyer-turned-evangelist; William and Catherine Booth, who founded the Salvation Army, now the largest charitable organization in the world; and Billy Graham, counselor and confidant of eleven U.S. presidents, who preached God's unconditional love and saving grace to millions. Liardon goes beyond history, drawing crucial life application and inspiration from the lives of these mighty warriors.

ISBN: 978-1-60374-025-8 • Hardcover • 496 pages

www.whitakerhouse.com

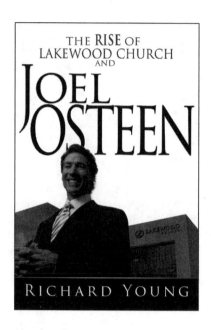

The Rise of Lakewood Church and Joel Osteen
Richard Young

He was the most unlikely of protégés—a young man with no college or seminary degree and virtually no preaching experience. Yet, Joel Osteen was handed the reigns of his father's lifelong ministry when John Osteen died suddenly in 1999. Witness the miraculous rise of Lakewood Church from humble beginnings in a Texas feed store to becoming the largest church in America. Learn the inside story that catapulted Joel Osteen to prominence as one of the most influential Christian voices of our generation. From the life and times of John and Joel Osteen you will learn the power of vision, humility, integrity, and facing adversity with faith. Never again will you doubt what God can do with those who are fully devoted to Him!

ISBN: 978-0-88368-975-2 • Hardcover • 272 pages

www.whitakerhouse.com